Squatting London

'A timely and urgent book that challenges how we come to think about property and homeownership while reminding us that there are other ways – makeshift, precarious and subversive – of inhabiting and transforming the city. *Squatting London* chronicles the everyday actions of the city's diverse squatter community and the alternative urban landscape that they have come to assemble and cultivate.'

—Alexander Vasudevan, author of *The Autonomous City: A History of Urban Squatting*

'Who deserves space? Who is entitled to home? Squatting, Sam Burgum tells, flips dominant propertied scripts, insisting that home should be linked to use, rather than privilege. In a powerful and subversive account, Burgum opens up the political space of the city as he takes us inside London's squats.'

—Nicholas Blomley, Professor of Geography, Simon Fraser University

'The generative power of squatting lies at the core of the stories, people and places narrated in Burgum's beautiful book. If one takes squatting not just as a site of politics, but as a productive infrastructure enabling for multiple forms of the political to flourish and become, then one sees the role squats plays in enriching the grounds upon which the many – not just squatters – can struggle for more just housing and cities. *Squatting London* is a forceful call to take such agenerative power seriously and an important resource to work with it.'

—Michele Lancione, author of *For a Liberatory Politics of Home*

'Homes without people, people without homes. This book demonstrates that squatting is not just the correction of this unfair mathematics, but also the creation of collectivity and a generation of political subjects in a context of social disregard and dispossession.'

—Raquel Rolnik, author of *Urban Warfare: Housing and Cities in the Age of Finance*

'Contemporary squatting research has long needed an analytically grounded ethnography of squatters themselves. Burgum has listened to the voices we need to hear. In sophisticated reflections on their experiences, these London squatters tell of the elation of being with a crew acting for the common good, and the fragility of lumpen collectives. It's an invaluable snapshot of a ground-level social movement among the most deprived elements of a western society.'

—Alan W. Moore, author of *Occupation Culture: Art & Squatting in the City from Below*

'A remarkable theatrical ethnography, whose author Samuel Burgum trespasses in revolutionary territories. Meeting deep material, social, political and cultural needs, the squat is a question mark for property owners – and more-than-imaginary stepping stone to communing.'

—Anitra Nelson, author of *Beyond Money: A Postcapitalist Strategy*

'Burgum seamlessly merges activist and academic accounts as he provides a thought-provoking overview of the various left-wing squatters and squatted projects which continue to exist in the cracks of contemporary, gentrified London.'

—E.T.C. Dee, author of *Squatting the Grey City*

Squatting London

The Politics of Property

Samuel Burgum

First published 2025 by Pluto Press
New Wing, Somerset House, Strand, London WC2R 1LA
and Pluto Press, Inc.
1930 Village Center Circle, 3-834, Las Vegas, NV 89134

www.plutobooks.com

British Library Cataloguing in Publication Data
A catalogue record for this book is available from the British Library

ISBN 978 0 7453 4143 9   Paperback
ISBN 978 1 78680 828 8   PDF
ISBN 978 1 78680 829 5   EPUB

This book is printed on paper suitable for recycling and made from fully managed
and sustained forest sources. Logging, pulping and manufacturing processes are
expected to conform to the environmental standards of the country of origin.

Typeset by Stanford DTP Services, Northampton, England

Simultaneously printed in the United Kingdom and United States of America

Contents

Acknowledgements

I am indebted to London's squatters. Even those who decided *not* to share their stories were keen to help me learn and understand. For those who did participate, I hope you feel your generous donation of time was worthwhile and that I have given a fair portrayal. Thank you especially to those who made the project possible by facilitating introductions and vouching for me.

I am grateful for the Leverhulme Trust funding (ECF-2017-191) I received between 2017 and 2020, which gave me the space and time to carry out this project. I would like to thank Rowland Atkinson, who supported me to develop the bid and then the project when I joined the Urban Studies & Planning Department at the University of Sheffield. I also found vital support at the Urban Institute and especially the urban studies ECR network.

I am very fortunate to be working alongside some inspiring colleagues. I would like to thank Alex Vasudevan for his encouraging feedback on the manuscript, as well as Elsa Noterman, Kesia Reeve, Isabella Pojuner, Ryan Powell, Nathan Kerrigan, and Zaki Nahaboo, for helping me develop my thinking here. This work has also been shaped by the activists and researchers I met at SqEK (Squatting Europe Kollective) convergences in Catania in 2018 and Madrid in 2019.

I am thankful for my parents Paul and Julia, and to Val. Finn, thank you for giving me feedback on drafts and keeping me going with your endless support, love, and care. Writing and research can be a selfish thing and you've had to put up with a lot. This book is dedicated to Ezra – which means 'helper' in Hebrew – and a generation who will have no choice but to find spaces for radical change.

Staying Alert in Newham

Figure 1   'Better to Squat than Let Homes Rot: Resist Evictions' (Newham, 2019)
Source: Photo by the author.

We were already halfway across the road and the car had to brake hard. The driver waved us on, but I wondered what he must have thought as he witnessed the struggle. At face value, I expect he just took pity on us. The shopping trolly had a dodgy wheel and a pile of large razor-sharp metal sheets laid across the top. Flapping like giant silver wings on each side, they shifted balance every time a wheel hit a curb or pothole and it took immense concentration just to stop the whole lot tipping over. Perhaps the anonymous driver in a shirt and tie with a flashy German car was a landlord, I speculated. Perhaps he worked in real estate, an intermediary in London's vast financial sector, a bank, or a law firm. Yet here he was giving way to materials destined to barricade a squat.

That morning, I had met Oz at his new place: a long-abandoned charity shop on Forest Gate high street. The ground floor was typical for a squat, with bikes at various stages of repair, old sofas, office chairs, as well as other

Figure 2   Alert in Newham (Newham, 2019)
Source: Photo by the author.

potentially useful items liberated from skips and bins. Upstairs, the former offices had been repurposed as bedrooms and, as a bonus, there was even a working toilet. At the front, the squatter crew had somehow managed to get the shop shutter to work, which came down just behind the entrance. However, this would not be enough to resist eviction and, judging by the banner hanging outside, they intended to take a very public stand against the bailiffs.

Squatting is a way to create space in a city that is, at best, indifferent to those without money to rent or own property. At its worst, London is a proactively violent city, un-homing and displacing communities through a property system that excludes, divides, and denies people the spaces they need for housing or community. For Oz, squatting is simply a direct response to this context:

It's reclaiming space that is otherwise not used and putting it to use. When something's been left to rot, even if you believe in private property to some degree, those kinds of spaces should be reclaimed and put back into community use and for the public good.

I'd been promised a tour of some local squats, but first: the barricade. Oz knew of a large building round the corner which had been squatted

Figure 3 The Salvation Army (Newham, 2019)
Source: Photo by the author.

and was rumoured to have a large supply of Sitex. These perforated metal sheets were more commonly used to keep squatters *out* of vacant property, but his plan was to use their own technology against them. We grabbed the trolly and knocked on the door. Eventually a suspicious voice responded from inside and, after Oz explained that his group were looking for help to resist an impending eviction, the door slowly opened. As it turned out, while this person and Oz were strangers to each other, they knew a squatter in common, which helped establish some trust. We headed to a car park round the back where there were a few broken-down vans and beat-up caravans. After the sheets were loaded, and the conspicuous journey back to the charity shop was completed, we spent a sunny afternoon wandering around Newham, drinking cans of Polish lager, and dropping in on various squats.

London's squatting scene today is certainly not on the scale it was in the 1970s, nor as public as it was between the 1980s and the introduction of new police powers in 2012. 'I was around before the law change', said Oz, 'and most of the people who were, like, heavily involved have since moved on … there's simply been a massive change in the scene.' Yet cases keep cropping up, igniting public debates around vacancy, ownership, housing crisis, and entitlement in the city. As we walked around Newham, we called

Figure 4 'Love is in the heart' (Newham, 2019)
Source: Photo by the author.

in on some neighbouring squats, including an abandoned Salvation Army building. Here, the crew were halfway through moving house. They had been told that if they left voluntarily the charity would turn the building into sheltered accommodation for people facing street homelessness.

'Some people are squatters just because they have literally no other option,' Oz explained:

> Many of the people I know could go and get jobs … soul-destroying jobs to earn minimum wage. Even being paid minimum wage these days people struggle to pay rent for something that's not a fucking damp hole in the ground. It's a choice and a necessity. [But] for some people, it's only a necessity.

Having moved to London from abroad, Oz had originally stayed in people's houses, sofa-surfing while he was looking for a job and somewhere to rent. Where he came from, there wasn't really a squatting scene, but growing-up he had been involved in various punk houses, 'so it was actually on my radar':

> It was while I was still looking for somewhere to live and I met a couple of punks in Camden and they invited me back to their place. After hanging

Figure 5   Home (Newham, 2019)
Source: Photo by the author.

out with them for a while, over the course of a month, a place [squat] opened up and they invited me to come and move in. Then I witnessed first-hand immediately what goes because we were evicted five days later and had to open a new building! (laughs)

Occasionally, landlords in London do informally negotiate with squatters, seeing it as a way to get free security for their empty property. But this can depend on how the property owner perceives a particular crew and squatting in general. There is a tendency, for example, to characterise squatters as either 'good' (i.e. genuinely in desperate need of shelter) or 'bad' (i.e. lazy, layabouts, workshy, criminal, ideological). But for Oz, himself an experienced squatter, the situation on the ground was always much more complex than these stereotypes implied:

The point is not 'good squatters/bad squatters'. It's simply recognising that there are different circumstances. I think squatting is not one thing. It's not directly related to, say, anarchist principles (but there are a lot of people within the community who hold those principles). The idea of reclaiming space is an attack on private property. It's not about good

Figure 6 An evicted squat where the landlord appears to have left the windows open – Oz tells me this is an attempt to deter further squatting by encouraging deterioration and allowing pests in (Newham, 2019)

Source: Photo by the author.

squat or bad squat, there are just some dickheads you know who don't give a fuck, what can you do with them?'

Oz's own use of empty buildings was multifaceted, but he was keen to emphasise that different buildings were suitable for different purposes, depending on their material layout, but also on their location. Since 2012, and the criminalisation of trespassing in a residential building with the intention to reside, commercial spaces – offices, shops, pubs, warehouses – are now the only type of property where trespassing to 'reside' didn't automatically mean a criminal offence (although what counts as 'residing' or 'a residential property' is a grey area). Some squats are simply used as a temporary shelter – providing a momentary safety net for care, respite, and stability – others provide a temporary location from which squatters can find free time to participate in local campaigns, poorly paid jobs, or voluntary charity work, as well as London's underground subcultures. Oz told me:

I had no knowledge of ASS [Advisory Service for Squatters] or anything like that when I first arrived. Simply yeah ... went to a punk gig and met

Figure 7 An evicted squat where the landlord appears to have removed the roof –
Oz tells me this makes the space unliveable, but also creates neighbourhood blight
in anticipation of easily obtaining planning permission to demolish and regenerate
(Newham, 2019)

Source: Photo by the author.

some people there who invited me up to their squat for a party. [I was attracted by] the affiliation of people, of different types of people, you know? I never discussed kind of like, 'wider politics' in my younger years to that kind of degree ... [but squatting] drew me instantly.

Oz's crew that he was currently squatting with were opening up unused buildings for community use. As part of an ethics of solidarity, squatting was a tool for them to create spaces, both for the local neighbourhood and networks across the city:

We had a building on the high street. Opened it up every week ... well, in fairness, every day to anyone on the street, you know. Every week we would do a community ... we'd put on just like open mic things and people would just get to sing whatever they wanted and feel like they had a place to go. It was a community centre that just simply didn't exist otherwise, other than like sort of homeless shelters or whatever, you know? It was a place where you could get some food and chill out, hang out, and people loved it.

Having a 'public squat', however, also meant announcing their presence, which could create potential problems. While a crew might be motivated to open up spaces for community use, the presence of banners, graffiti, posters, or simply someone who 'looks like a squatter' going in or out of the building, was a signal to neighbours who might or might not be sympathetic, inviting potential criticism, police attention, or occasionally violence (such as from far-right groups). 'I can't pretend we [resist evictions] all the time,' explained Oz. 'It really depends who you're living with and what kind of place you're in ...'

It also is maybe that you actually just want a place for housing yourself. If we stay in this place longer, it will allow us more flexibility to do other projects and things like that. 'So, let's stay low on this one.' It really comes down to the situation, you know? There's places where we've immediately just hung up the banners and being like 'yes, we are a presence here' and other places that we don't. It depends on the make-up of the people you're with. What you set out to do.

You might be in a place with good people who simply don't want to draw attention to themselves. Squatting ... at the end of the day, you can say every act of squatting is political because its reappropriation of land that was enclosed. But for some people ... they're just getting a roof over their head and that in itself is also important. If we're going to consider everyone, we can't just be like: 'You need to be there putting up banner and fighting police.'

Three days after our walk around Newham, I heard a rumour that Oz's squat had been evicted. I sent a message asking if everything was alright and he responded:

Hey dude, yea we got chucked out, dozens of police in full riot gear, helmets and shields etc, not much we could do but held them off for half an hour, then I got nicked [arrested]. Released an hour ago with no charges.

He had been accused of setting off a fire extinguisher in the face of a police officer who was trying to break down the barricade. The officer, however, had no evidence. Besides, once the squatters had been evicted, then the aim had been achieved from the landlord's perspective. A few days later, the crew had a new space anyway:

> Gorgeous place in fact. Got a nice backyard and nice neighbours, perfect for summer. Bit like being back in residential [pre-criminalisation] times :)

Introduction:
The London Underground

Perhaps you think you already know what squatting is, or the kind of people that squatters are. Whatever your view, it's important to recognise that our perspective on squatting has been 'fuelled by, and built upon, a media narrative which characterises squatters as organised gangs of thugs, layabouts, and revolutionary fanatics, parasites, invaders who steal people's homes'.[1] Squatters are repeatedly and deliberately portrayed as a direct threat to an imagined law-abiding and hard-working majority, because they are seen as taking something that isn't 'rightfully' theirs. Such stereotypes rarely capture the complexity of squatting on the ground, yet these 'property outlaws'[2] come to symbolise wider cultural norms as to what is (or is not) considered a 'proper' use of a space, as well as who is (or is not) considered a 'legitimate' user of a space. The language used around squatting reflects wider notions of property entitlement and the figure of the 'squatter' acts as 'a node where various values intersect regarding morality and legality'.[3] A news story about a 'squat' quickly turns into a conversation around deservedness: a focal point for reasserting what counts as legitimate property use and who is considered a threat towards that entitlement. It's no surprise, therefore, that the 'migrant squatter' has dominated the media over the last few decades. Intersecting with wider xenophobic and racist discourses about entitlement in an austerity-wracked, fearful, and unequal nation, 'migrants, one could say, are seen to squat the space of the country in much the same way that squatters illegitimately occupy the space of a building'.[4]

Our views on property entitlement, however, are far from set in stone and they have been shaped over time. For example, in May 1946, inspired by post-war occupations of vacant hotels in Glasgow and Edinburgh, as well as the Vigilantes who did the same in Brighton, around 30,000–40,000 families squatted empty military properties across the UK. On its own terms, this was an extraordinary example of a spontaneous and grassroots response to housing crisis, but what was perhaps even more incredible was that the 'public' response was 'uniformly sympathetic'.[5] At the end of the Second World War, ex-service personnel had been promised 'homes fit for heroes', yet many had found themselves returning to poor-quality urban housing stock. Frustration grew with the slow progress of a Labour government, who were prioritising quality over quantity, but who were also hamstrung by a lack of materials and skilled workforce to build new houses. And it was in this context that outlets such as *British Pathé* newsreels reported on the squatted military bases as proof that 'the Blitz spirit lives on', with even the *Daily Mail* seizing an opportunity to criticise Labour's socialist housing policy and celebrate the squatters' 'robust common sense'.[6] While major politicians such as Prime Minister Attlee and Aneurin Bevan were careful not to condone the squatting, other public figures were downright celebratory, such as Alderman Hennessy in Bristol, who argued that the squatting was 'requisitioning by the people', and the Labour MP for Stafford, who 'told a public meeting that the squatters were morally justified in taking the law into their own hands'.[7] There was also public sympathy on the ground. In Sheffield, a team sent to evict and demolish a squatted military camp refused to do so until the residents there were given proper alternative accommodation.

Such a positive and sympathetic response to the post-war squatting wave, however, began to wane in September 1946, when 1,000 individuals from working-class neighbourhoods squatted the Duchess of Bedford House in Kensington, north London. The luxury apartments had originally been requisitioned by the state to house Gibraltarian refugees and, after the war ended, the (Conservative) local authority had declined an opportunity to use them as emergency accommodation so they now lay empty. Yet, in contrast to the occupations of the military camps, when the squatters moved into the flats in Kensington, they were framed as going a step too far. The families on the bases were portrayed as upstanding, respectable, *legitimate* citizens who had been forced into this situation by desperation, and were therefore morally entitled to occupy damp, cold, and draughty disused military huts, with some setting up milk rounds, postal addresses, and even being incorporated into local authority housing stock. Yet, in Kensington, the police responded by preventing supplies from getting inside, before eventually forcing an eviction using a 'conspiracy to trespass' charge from the reign of King Richard II (repealed in 1977). The Labour government was careful to demonstrate public 'sympathy for 'ordinary people' seeking to put a roof over their head',[8] but the cabinet minutes reveal broad agreement that force might be necessary 'to secure respect for property', and predicting that there would not be the same public compassion for those squatting in Kensington as there had been for those in the military camps. This foreshadowed a similar narrative in 2017, when there were calls to requisition empty properties in Kensington after the Grenfell Tower fire.[9] These families were seen as 'illegitimate' users of property, taking something that they weren't entitled to and unfairly jumping the housing waiting list.

By investigating squatting today – while also considering both what it has been and what it could be – this book challenges preconceived ideas around who is or is not entitled to use space. Against a precarious and marginalising urban backdrop, squats both reveal and challenge property norms around how space is currently being unfairly distributed and used, especially in cities which have an overheated property landscape that is stifling for those pushed to the margins. Anyone familiar with contemporary London will know that cranes are a permanent fixture on the skyline, acting as trig-points of 'creative destruction', investment, gentrification, and social cleansing. Luxury skyscrapers continue to be piled high, leaving behind many thousands of homeless people and many thousands of people-less homes, while austerity and inflation have brought cuts to public services, institutions, and spaces, which formed the social safety net. Squats are a direct response to these contradictions. They are 'a way of obtaining what has been denied [and] a way to draw attention to the waste of public land and buildings and the high costs of building speculation'.[10] It is in London's empty buildings, behind boarded-up windows and doors with crowbar-bent corners, that a simple idea is being kept alive: the spaces we need are already all around us.

WHAT IS SQUATTING?

Squatting is a specific type of trespass of unused and wasted properties, motivated by an *ongoing* need for space. It is also a claim to space which seeks to justify itself through *use* rather than ownership or permission, arguing – through actions or words – that 'ownership of property was a secondary consideration to the fact that it is empty'.[11] In an era dominated by capitalist market exchange, land registers, property deeds, rental agreements, and commercial leases, the idea that 'use' is an acceptable claim to space has become alien. Yet there is a long and buried history of property in the UK in which use-claims were not only socially recognised, but even had a basis in law. In *Cotters and Squatters*, Colin Ward traces some of this forgotten archive, and comes to the conclusion that 'squatting is the oldest mode of tenure in the world and we are all descended from squatters'.[12] One example is the folklore of 'the one-night house' (also known as a 'Clod Hall' or 'Ty Unnos' in Wales), which was an 'old custom … whereby a person was entitled to the freehold of whatever shelter he or she could build in a night and of the land within a stone's throw'.[13] Realistically, it seems unlikely that the one-night house was literally built 'overnight'. But what this custom allowed was for some flexibility for local negotiation over who was entitled to claim unused spaces on the boundaries of formal property, repurposing the wastelands, heaths, moors, forests, and roadsides. According to Ward, 'the attitude of manorial courts towards squatter houses [likely] depended on such factors as the current demand for labour',[14] which meant that 'squatter cottages mushroomed in the wake of the industrial revolution'[15] as labourers 'settled strategically on the fringes ... to win a livelihood'.[16]

But even as recently as the 1960s, squatters in London had success in finding *legal* tools to validate their claim to a vacant property and challenge absent or neglectful owners. The London Squatters' Campaign emerged out of a series of homeless hostel occupations and a wave of public sympathy for precariously housed people (particularly after the airing of *Cathy Come Home* on public television). The campaigners planned to test what the police, courts, media, and public would consider acceptable by moving poorly housed families into empty council houses in Redbridge, London. In *The Squatters*, Ron Bailey[17] reflects on the laws they anticipated might be used against them. Because their intent was for the family to *reside* in the property, they reasoned that they couldn't be charged with 'breaking and entering'. However, there was an outside chance they could be arrested for riotous and unlawful assembly, including a breach of the peace. Furthermore, although trespass was (and still is) a civil offence in England and Wales, they were also aware of the 'conspiracy to trespass' charge, which had been used against the Kensington squatters in 1946 (although this had never actually been tested in court). Related offences might also include theft if they used utilities without paying, so they planned to take meter readings and register with water and electricity companies as soon as they got in.

Their wager was that they could win a moral argument: that owners' entitlement to vacant properties should not be respected above their potential to be used as homes. During the first squats in 1969, they even echoed the language which had surrounded the post-war squatters, arguing these were just ordinary people in need of homes and who were being let down by an inefficient state and market. When the bailiffs came, among them members of the fascist National Front, the squatters publicised the brutality and violence of an attempted eviction, before seeking legal support for the squats through the courts. It was here that an important legal precedent was established. While the Forcible Entry Acts of 1381 and 1429 made it an offence to take possession of land by force, the London Squatters Campaign wagered that they could use this law *in their favour* because, by securing the premises, it would then be the bailiffs who would be using force to evict *them*:

> The law is quite clear: one must not enter and repossess land without a court order 'with strong hand or multitude of people', even if one has a legal right of entry. The reason for this law is that private individuals should not be allowed to employ armies to fight over land, but that disputes should be settled through the courts which will repossess the land for the rightful party.[18]

This is an early example of the way in which squatters continue to 'invest time and energy in trading with the enemy, assuming the practices and knowledge needed to keep them squatting lawfully'.[19] What became known as 'squatters rights' ensured 'that owners seeking eviction went through the courts, affording squatters a minimal degree of security without which squatting could not have gone beyond the stage of protest sit-ins'.[20] Though not 'legally entirely correct',[21] 'squatters rights' refers to this legal precedent that squatters have been able to mobilise in asserting and defending their legitimate use of a vacant space over that of an owner. However, this tended to only delay eviction rather than allow for a longer-term use of a space. What's more, since the Criminal Law Act 1977 – which introduced new powers to crack down on squatting and which was passed the same year as the Greater London Council's squatter amnesty, which incorporated squatters into the housing system – the moral and legal argument for squatting has been increasingly undermined.

As Finchett-Maddock has argued, from 1977 onwards, 'immorality is always on the side of the squatter' which has had a knock-on effect of drawing 'our attention away from the responsibility that might be apportioned to the property owners'.[22] Through the development of greater legal protections, property owners have been increasingly enabled to remove themselves from the notion that they should be putting a building into use or risk losing it. Historically, the question of who was the legitimate user of a space was seen as a direct conflict 'between the owner and the squatter, to be resolved using the civil law toolkit', but the steady intervention of criminal law has meant that 'squatting has been redefined as a crime against the state, requiring public punishment, retribution, and censure'.[23] This shifts any conversation or contestation over legitimate use *away* from the actual situation on the ground and notions of use and justice, allowing owners to disregard any 'ethical argument that landowners bear a duty of effective stewardship, to satisfy the wider public or community interest in effective land use'.[24]

As Nick Wates recognised, way back in 1976, when reflecting on the squats involved in *The Battle for Tolmers Square*:

> [Whether] an owner can obtain a possession order against squatters or not has nothing to do with whether he has any alternative use for the property, or whether the squatters will become homeless as a result ... moral and political questions do not enter into it ... the owner merely has to fulfil a number of legal technicalities.[25]

> the property system does not look upon land and property as an asset in any environmental or social sense ... it is a financial asset, and the location and character of development are not determined by usefulness or social need, but by a profit and loss account.[26]

The decline of moral and legal precedent for use-claims has been paralleled by greater moral and legal protections for owners. Since at least the Limitation Act 1623 there has been a legal principle that property ownership should not simply go unlimited and uncontested,[27] yet the idea of responsible property use, as well as the importance of use value over exchange value, has been steadily undermined by the consolidation of the ownership model and a shift 'from factual possession to registration'.[28] For example, while the Limitation Act 1980 re-established the principle that someone in possession of a property could claim adverse possession and become the legal owner after 12 years (if the registered owner didn't object until that point); the Land Registration Act 2002 made it compulsory for an adverse possessor (i.e. squatter) to apply to the Land Registry, before then giving the registered owner the right to refuse. This is part of a long trend of formalising property since at least the Land Registry Act 1862, which aimed 'to give certainty to the title of real estates and to facilitate the proof thereof'[29] and, since 1925, the 'aim of a complete tabular register of all estates in land within England and Wales, following from the "Torrens system" as seen in [colonial] Australia and other common law as well as civil law jurisdictions'.[30]

This book shows how squatting, as a form of trespass, continues to challenge existing entitlements based solely upon ownership, in favour of reasserting the importance of use. As an example of 'efficient trespass',[31] each squat raises questions around whose possession of space is legitimate and who gets to decide. Moments of trespass always provide us with 'a window onto the politics of property at a given moment in a given social context',[32] and 'the history of squatting is in part a history of competing attempts to define legitimate claims on land, using both the law and the court of public opinion'.[33] It is through trespass that a property regime is forced to reassert itself, reveal its true colours, and demonstrate its absurdity. When a squat happens, it unveils hoarded unused spaces, as well as the mechanisms through which they are being protected, defended, and policed. Simply through their actions, squatters repeatedly demonstrate 'that there remain substantial opportunities for creative, disruptive, transformative social action, within which the very meaning of value (and with it, citizenship and property) is contested and redefined'.[34]

Squatting is both an outcome of the dominance of ownership, which restricts access to space, but also a direct challenge to it. Every squat asserts a right to use a particular space, simply by utilising, defending, and negotiating that use at ground level, rather than deferring to legal systems of ownership. In doing so, squatters put forward an argument that their need for space – which is not otherwise being fulfilled or recognised – is legitimate. Whoever we are, our needs for space are diverse and inconsistent. They change over time in response to personal circumstances as well as ever-shifting political trends and economic conditions. Whether or not we can access suitable spaces to match our needs, for example, has an obvious role to play in how we use, and who can use, space. What's more, each building has property norms baked into the concrete – planning permissions, intended purpose, target audience (which dictates layout, size, location, price), present condition – all of which are context-dependent. Over time, squatters have become experts at adapting and manipulating vacant buildings which were meant for other (more profitable) purposes. However, they still come up against material limits, such as trying keep a warehouse warm enough to sleep in or attempting to open up a social centre in a long-neglected space only to discover damp, mould, or asbestos. As the stigma which surrounds squatting demonstrates, these conditions align with moral judgements as to what is considered a 'proper' use of space or a 'legitimate' user of space. Squatters, of course, routinely come into dispute with landlords, police, and neighbours over their intended (re)use of a space, as well as argue with each other. The real problem of property, therefore, is who gets to decide? By what authority? And how are prevailing ideas of 'acceptable' use negotiated or challenged?

THE POLITICS OF PROPERTY

Ownership is the fantasy that we can have a direct relationship with some-thing in our possession (i.e. *'this is mine!'*). In practice, property is always a relationship *between people*, often mediated by the law and/or violence, which is constantly being re-performed (i.e. *'this is mine, not yours'* or *'this is ours, not theirs'*). And yet the illusion of the ownership model of property[35] has a 'powerful imaginative hold' which shapes 'our understandings of the possibilities of social life, the ethics of human relations and the ordering of economic life ... property becomes simply (and ... frighteningly) taken for granted'.[36] Whether or not an owner is entitled to their property, there-fore, largely goes unquestioned. The aim of ownership is to shut down competing use-claims, or difficult questions around social justice, simply by refusing to entertain any claims that fall outside of title or permission. When owners defer to the state to defend their entitlement, the everyday relationships between people with regard to using space become alienated and obscured. Disagreements over what a space *should* be used for become 'settled in advance', thereby denying and ignoring the ways in which 'people lay claim to property in much more varied, overlapping and often collec-tively oriented ways'.[37] Rather than the democratic messiness of agreement, disagreement, negotiation, conflict, compromise, and division; the owner-ship model simply refuses to recognise property as a social relation.

To begin with, however, even the ownership model of property had to justify itself through 'use'. When political philosopher John Locke argued that the enclosure of land could only be justified if that property was put to 'higher and better use' and that 'as much and as good was left to others', this allowed ownership to shroud itself in a moral cloak. Under settler coloni-alism, 'highest and best use' was something solely attributed to European uses of space, and not existing indigenous uses of space. This enabled white settlers to rationalise their claiming of land through exclusion and violence, using a moral lens that they were putting empty spaces to 'better use'. As argued by Brenna Bhandar in *Colonial Lives of Property*, the ownership model is therefore rooted in racialising logics which pre-position who is or is not a legitimate user of space. The idea that white settlers could put land to 'higher and better use' was built upon a racist ideology that land requires improvement 'because its inhabitants are also in need of civilizational uplift, and vice versa'.[38] Such logics were also used during the height of land enclo-sures in the UK to provide reasoning for the loss of customary rights and the eviction of commoners, who were framed as immoral and incapable of 'improving' the land.[39]

There have even been examples where governments have *encouraged* squatting through this Lockean reasoning. Using the common law principle of adverse possession – where occupying unused land for a certain amount of time would allow the trespasser to gain title to it – the US government sought to expand settlement further west where land had been 'claimed' by colonists but had gone 'unused'. The Homestead Act 1862 allowed those who squatted plots of land in order to put it into 'productive use' to then claim title to that land, which itself is a clear example of the inherent problem at the heart of Locke's argument. While, on the surface, putting disused space into 'use' could be considered a progressive way to manage who can or cannot use it, this also leaves unexamined assumptions of what (or who) *counts* as 'the highest and best use', which is far from objective, often violent, and built upon exclusionary histories such as race, class, gender, and impairment.

In contrast, however, claiming adverse possession in the courts has also been used by squatters in order to defend their use of a space against eviction by the state and/or an (en)titled owner. In her work with a community that occupied and gardened disused land in Philadelphia, Elsa Noterman has argued that adverse possession may well have enrolled the gardeners 'in normative property regimes', but it also gave them the 'potential to resist these regimes through errant performances' of property.[40] In this sense, she argues that adverse possession has the *potential* to be used strategically and to hold on to 'space for tactical intervention in processes of enclosure, while acknowledging important critiques of urban commons in the context of ongoing dispossession and "racial banishment" in settler colonial cities'.[41] Through the process of claiming adverse possession, Noterman argues that the squatters were forced to act '"as if" they were private property owners to ward off enclosure' *but also* '"as if" urban commons were broadly valued and recognisable'.[42] The strategic use of adverse possession, in other words, allowed the gardeners to defend their ongoing use of the property, even though they had to seek ownership in order to do so.

Yet there are also examples where the use of adverse possession has created new challenges between the squatters themselves. In *Ours to Lose*, Amy Starecheski traces the extraordinary history of squatters in New York City. Until 1974, the city government supported an 'urban homesteading' housing programme, which sought to encourage self-reliance, individual responsibility, and citizenship, through 'sweat equity'. The idea was that individuals could claim property title if they renovated an empty space and lived there for at least five years. This was a win-win for the city, as it was a cheap way to provide housing to low- and moderate-income communities, while also bringing disused City-owned land into the market through ownership. But when New York went bankrupt in the mid-1970s, the programme was defunded, just as landlords began to abandon buildings in unprofitable (poor) neighbourhoods. On the lower east side, some communities responded by squatting. Justifying their occupation as carrying forward the spirit of the urban homesteading programme, they also positioned themselves as protecting the buildings from others that they saw as 'illegitimate' users, such as drug addicts, sex workers, and dossers.

When capital returned to the city in the 1980s, squatters then sought to protect their ongoing property use through adverse possession, but soon found out how difficult this could be. Not only did their case require the US legal system to recognise wider moral and political claims to property; it also required squatters themselves to judge claims to space *internally*. In seeking to formalise their use, conflicts began to emerge between those who had originally occupied the building, restored it, and put a 'new door' on the front, versus those who had lived in the building, but were perceived as not having contributed (either because they were 'dossers', or because they were unable to). Moving towards the ownership model, in other words, produced 'new persons: new leaders, new winners, and new losers in the ongoing struggle for space in the squats'[43] and 'as they became homeowners the pressure to somehow articulate their values with those of private property and neoliberal capitalism became intense'.[44] 'Before legalisation', Starecheski observes, 'a building could more easily accommodate the different work patterns of those working for ownership and those looking for raw shelter ... the previously unquantifiable but not unnoticed debts between members were now being quantified and written down.'[45]

This is a clear example of how property relations are *social*. As a relationship between people towards a valued resource, it is not just a matter of how squatters come into contact with owners or the state, it is also about how they handle their own interpersonal relationships towards the space. Squatting – in contrast to the ownership model – holds open the possibility for agreement and disagreement, negotiation and conflict, compromise and division. Squatters tend not to presume that legitimate use can *only* be decided by title or contract and instead make localised claims to legitimate property use. Rather than shutting down debate over how a space should be used or who should use it by deferring to the abstract and exclusionary authority of the ownership model, squatting has the *potential* to be more inclusive. By definition, squatters cannot claim authority for their use from a legal title. As such, they are forced into an imminent and material negotiation around who has a legitimate claim to use a squatted space, or for what purposes a squat should (or should not) be used. Legitimate use is constantly performed, which permits the very messiness that the ownership model was designed to avoid.

Because it goes unquestioned, property becomes depoliticised under the ownership model. In contrast, however, squatters (as well as other trespassers) put social relations back on the table. By emphasising use over registration, they question and undermine the automatic power of registered ownership (particularly if owners are negligent and are hoarding or wasting valuable resources). They ensure that 'the rights conferred by title are never unlimited', reminding us that 'while rights in property may seem to simply come from possession of legal title ... [they] are grounded also in social responsibility'.[46] The question that squatters raise again and again is whether ownership should be the *only* way to decide legitimate use. What's more, because it is localised, squatting also harbours the potential to allow for greater flexibility in directly meeting needs on a local level. In contrast to ownership, squatting keeps property relations open and grounded. This, of course, means dealing with conflict, disagreement, and power dynamics, but it can also facilitate routes to social justice by potentially allowing for plasticity, negotiation, inclusion, and compromise.

WHY SQUATTING MATTERS

With 36,210 empty homes,[47] London has the highest proportion of unoccupied residential buildings across all the regions in England (8% of all homes in the city), the vast majority of which (91.6%) are thought to be truly vacant (i.e. where no one lives for more than 30 days per year).[48] Even before we take into account other types of under-used property – such as vacant commercial property and undeveloped 'brownfield' sites – there is more than enough vacant space in London, and yet people still struggle to access the spaces they need. In the 'post-crisis' urban landscape – after the 2008 crash, neoliberal austerity, the pandemic, recessions, inflation, and the cost-of-living crisis – there is an anti-social abundance of empty buildings. Either through the simple pursuit of the highest return on investment in a property, or through the speculative warehousing of valuable land, capitalism incentivises building for profit rather than for use. Squatting is an example of urban vitality which scratches out spaces in the face of an indifferent and violent system. Through their creative actions, squatters force us to rethink property and rethink the city. Shops closed for business become social centres. Abandoned restaurants become spaces for hosting experimental art exhibitions. Empty offices become bedrooms. Dusty warehouses become places to gather. Closed public libraries become sites to protest public funding cuts. Pubs, clinics, youth clubs, sports halls, garden centres, car parks, wasteland, are being spontaneously developed from below. By doing so, squatters are collectively maintaining, reinventing, and perpetuating urban life from behind the scenes.

As ethnographic research, this book incorporates archival work, observations of squatted spaces, as well as interviews and photo-elicitation interviews, focusing on the granular, everyday experiences of the urban margins in London. Rather than seeing squats as chaotic, peripheral, and inconsequential, the aim is to 'speak to a range of spatial grammars of occupation which harness the political potential of the city by "staying close" to the messiness of urban life'.[49] In this way, I have sought to pay attention to the 'propositional politics of liminal spaces'[50] and 'the city yet to come'[51] by platforming squats as creative, imaginative, and aspirational parts of the city. The insights described might therefore have significance for property norms which echo in many other cities, forcing us to contend with and question the ownership model of property in myriad ways, raising questions as to how urban spaces are distributed, managed, and controlled. In particular, my objective was to learn about the challenge of property relations in practice (both between squatters and the ownership model, but also with one another). This book has plenty of examples where squats have acted as a crucial lifeline, a 'level before the street', a 'safety net below the safety net', a place of warmth, camaraderie, and collective belonging. Squats are overlooked corners of the city, but they are also indispensable 'structures of feeling' and 'sources of care, refuge and solidarity', even while they are being rendered 'fragmentary and precarious'.[52] Taking my lead from those squatters who participated, this is not a romanticised account of such spaces.

Accessing an underground scene is difficult. I started by getting back in touch with participants who were part of my research with Occupy (in) London, but I also relied heavily on the willingness of squatters to vouch for me. Except for 'open' squats, such as parties or exhibitions, I made it a rule not to cold-call and just turn up at the door. Instead, I would only visit if I had been invited by one of the crew in that building, however this didn't necessarily mean that others had been informed or were happy with me being there. This of course raises ethical issues which chime with questions around property, entitlement, and who has authority to decide who is invited or excluded from spaces. The photo-elicitation interviews were an attempt to decentre myself in the narrative. Disposable cameras were handed out to squatters, with minimal instructions (so as not to influence what they considered to be significant). This was then followed by an interview on the photographs, which allowed participants to tell me what *they* considered to be important about the space. All gave signed permission for their photographs to be published here, however any in which people could be identified have not been used. I was accused more than once of being an undercover police officer (which is unsurprising given the UK government's ongoing use of such tactics).[53] However, there were no incidents where I was asked to leave, and usually any situation de-escalated quickly when my host explained who I was. I made an active effort to introduce myself and the project to everyone in a space, but inevitably this wasn't always practical. I therefore kept my observations reserved to the space itself and only took photographs with permission, and in which people couldn't be identified. Where photos published in the book risk giving away the location of a squat, those spaces are no longer occupied (as far as I am aware).

Despite decades of smears targeted towards social research, as well as a general decline of critical thinking and the university sector, I still believe that we can be useful. Not only do we (sometimes) have privileged access to money, time, and space to learn and communicate, but we are also 'required to think systematically while locating human experience at the core ... combin[ing] abstract and grounded local registers to grapple with the causal factors that accentuate and sustain these problems'.[54] It's quite right that we are challenged, denied, and pushed back by people who distrust our motives or who don't see the point of what we doing. But this doesn't mean that we should give up and I agree with the argument that 'creative and socially relevant research agendas' are 'capable of bringing what are often concealed or invisible social problems to light',[55] and that 'sociology, if nothing else, provides us with a setting for conjecture and debate as to who we are and how we want to live'.[56]

Each chapter begins with a contradiction and a challenge that squatters raise around what London is and what it could be, including: the housing crisis, who has the right to be in the city, the politics of aspiration and change, and the creative importance of art, culture, and new ideas.

Chapter 1 focuses on housing crisis. Squatters may be more or less desperate to squat, and levels of desperation could also easily change for individuals at different stages in their life, but what squatters expressed

across the research was above all a desire to free up their time and participate in non-profitable activity *instead* of working in poor-quality jobs just
to pay the ridiculously high rent required to live in the capital (which I call
the wage–rent vortex). With the loss of state funding from public welfare,
including the decline in socially funded housing, I was told multiple times
that squatting is a 'safety net below the safety net'. Rather than live a soulless
existence working just to meet the cost of living, squatting created the space
and time squatters needed, not only to stay put but also to find purpose,
freedom, and meaning.

In chapter 2, the focus is on using squatting to stay located in the city.
By asserting their right to be in, use, and participate in an urban community, squatters also raise wider questions around who has the right to be in
the city in the first place and who gets to decide. Against centrifugal market
forces of regeneration and gentrification which are spinning people out of
London, squatting asserts a right to stay put. I argue that these examples
represent a 'squatter citizenship' or a defiant domesticity, in the face of an
ownership model that would deny them location, participation in, and recognition as part of the city.

Squatting also forces us to ask what kind of society we aspire to be. In
chapter 3, I frame squats as an infrastructure for political networks that work
across different scales, offering platforms which simultaneously centre and
decentre political campaigns. I show how it's meaningless to try to separate
the means and the ends, the political and non-political, because squats are
always engaging with, shaping, and shaped by, their wider context.

Finally, in chapter 4, I use the example of art and cultural activity within
squats to ask whether creativity and new ideas are given any room in the city.
I make the case that squats are important for art and culture, freeing up time
to be unprofitable, facilitating new ways to be part of something in common,
as well as providing access to arts and culture for those who are not from a
privileged class background (i.e. with money and 'taste'). Such spaces are
also crucial for providing a toolkit and a platform for being heard and seen.

Each chapter title is a double take – 'the politics of location, the location
of politics'; 'an aspiration for space, a space for aspiration'; and 'making space
for art, the art of making space' – inspired by a banner which circulated
around occupations at the Sweets Way and Carpenters housing estates in
2015: 'these people need homes, these homes need people'. Squatting encap-
sulates and responds to both sides of each chapter heading. It is a way of
connecting homeless people with people-less homes. It is a way of staying
located and part of the city – a 'squatter citizen' – as well as a way of estab-

lishing locations from which political arguments against dislocation can be made. It is an aspiration to make space within a property system that denies access to this fundamental resource, but also a space from which aspirations for an alternative society can be articulated. Finally, it is a way of making room for art, creativity, and expression for those who would not otherwise have the means for such meaningful (but also unprofitable) activities. In distinction to the criticism that squatters are scroungers who want 'something for nothing', I argue that squats matter because they turn 'nothing into *something*'.

Solidarity on Great Portland Street

Figure 8   Sofia House on Great Portland Street (Westminster, 2018)
Source: Photo by the author.

Whether through negotiation or via the crowbar, Streets Kitchen find ways to access disused spaces for setting up refuges and solidarity hubs. By doing so, in the context of widespread homelessness *and* vacant buildings across London, they also *politicise* these spaces. In March 2018, facing the possibility of widespread deaths on the streets of London, they responded in characteristic fashion by squatting 'Sofia House' – an empty commercial building on Great Portland Street. An unseasonal weather front dubbed 'the Beast from the East' saw heavy snow and icy winds sweep across the UK. Temperatures in London struggled to climb above -14°C, prompting a 'Red Snow Warning' and possible risk to life. Yet the response from local authorities was inconsistent and patchy. The idea behind the Severe Weather Emergency Protocol (SWEP) is to coordinate a city-wide response to provide shelters, yet there always seems to be some reluctance to announce SWEP 'too early'. A combination of public funding cuts (austerity), and different political ideologies (empathies) towards 'the homeless', also means that

Figure 9   'You Can't Hide the Homeless' (Westminster, 2018)
Source: Photo by the author.

the availability of shelters varies massively across London. What's more, shelters simply aren't suitable for everyone. Some hate the feeling of being confined. Some distrust the state and fear giving over their personal details, which might expose their whereabouts to family members, or reveal their migration status in a hostile environment. The omnipresent St Mungo's had come under heavy criticism at the time for reporting people to the Home Office, while other bigger, more 'corporate' charities are often seen as disempowering 'service users', who must play the part of a desperate victim to be considered a suitable candidate for support.[1] This is why Streets Kitchen adopts the slogan: 'Solidarity Not Charity'.

Sofia House – squatted during a snowstorm – stood in clear contrast to the cold and inhospitable streets, but also the half-hearted, slow, and often alienating response of the state and the third sector. By just *doing* it, squatters make the question of how we match homeless people with peopleless homes simple, and their occupation clearly demonstrated the contradictions of space in London. 'You've got people sleeping outside empty buildings ... this is ridiculous', Yale argued:

> People should be in those buildings ... Even if it was only temporary. The perspective I'm coming from is to end rough sleeping *overnight*. Once we have those people into a safe space, we can work with those people, we can have the support services around it. But the primary thing we need is buildings. *The buildings are there!* ... We need councils to take

Figure 10   'Tents in the streets. £1,000,000 apartments left empty' (Euston Road, 2018)

Source: Photo by the author.

responsibility for those buildings and work with us. Working together is the solution we see … and, through Sofia House, we proved it can be done.

I first visited on the day they received an eviction order. None of the windows on the ground floor opened, and the only door – while regularly being opened by a steady flow of people coming in and out – was mostly being kept shut to retain heat and security. The smell of cigarette smoke, cooking, and the stale musk of hundreds of bodies that had slept here for weeks hung in the air. But it was warm. Some people were sleeping in rows. Others sat on sofas watching TV, chatting, or stood by the kitchen with a cup of tea, eyeing the donated food spread out for anyone to help themselves. To the left, there were rails of free clothes and an information stall, including a few copies of the *Squatters Handbook*.

Yale had a bit of a reputation for being determined and hardcore. When I found him, however, he was being accosted from all sides. Some of the people staying in the squat were anxious about the eviction notice and wanted to know how long they had. All around the room people had begun to pack their belongings with a sense that it was inevitable this day would come. There were also volunteers, journalists, and students, all trying to grab a minute with Yale to ask him questions. So, when I finally got my chance, I quickly introduced myself as a researcher before asking whether there was anything I could do to help. Rightly fed up with journalists and researchers, he snapped back: 'If you want to help, get a crowbar and open another fucking building!'

Figure 11 'Social Housing Not Social Cleansing' (Focus E15 Street Stall, 2018)
Source: Photo by the author.

We laughed about this a few months later. Yale told me it hadn't been long after my visit that they were evicted, but he didn't let people go away empty-handed:

> We gave people as they were leaving the opportunity ... crowbars for the next building ... or a good sleeping bag. They were the only options we could give. We couldn't give anybody a bed.

There had been a short-lived attempt to set up another squat. But, with the weather improving slightly, this wasn't as high-profile as Sofia House. I asked Yale why squatting wasn't more common given the availability of empty spaces and the clear need for them:

> There can be a fear of it. I mean squats are scary places ... you're going into a building ... I personally know it's all legal, legal, legal. But these people coming in are afraid of the system, they want to try and keep themselves on low profiles. They think if they go into that building it might affect them, or go against them ... Like, we found at Sofia [House]

Figure 12 'Considerate constructors build homes for people not for profit! Social housing now' (Temporary Autonomous Art – TAA, 2019)

Source: Photo by the author.

for the first few days, we had to show it was *us* doing it … that it was 'homeless-run' … to get people in.

For the same reasons that someone might be hesitant to approach charities or the state for shelter, it seems that many were also wary of Sofia House to begin with. To gain trust, Streets Kitchen knew they had to make it clear they were 'of' the community. Many of the volunteer crew had been through patches of sleeping rough, squatting, or general housing precarity, and this meant they could gain trust to establish a space of mutual support:

The model we're trying to create is a more-or-less open-door and we're going for the hardest to reach people. To get them through the door. That community's not being serviced. And it's through squats that we can do that. I think they'll trust a squat a lot more than a hostel.

Sofia House became more than simply a shelter for over 200 people to survive a snowstorm. Compared to the emergency SWEP shelters reluctantly opened by the state, this was a location for care and solidarity. Over

Figure 13 'Squat the lot' (TAA, 2018)
Source: Photo by the author.

the three weeks, 12 people were admitted straight to hospital for life-threatening conditions, while a further 50–60 were medically treated. Streets Kitchen were also able to pool, and make accessible, valuable resources, including food, clothes, and new sleeping bags (including a donation from Susan Sarandon).

There were some challenges that came with running an 'open-door' policy, and the crew coordinating the space took an active role in making sure the squat stayed safe:

> On duty, people would walk about at night. Because if you're sleeping amongst 200 people you don't know, it's nice to know that someone is walking about in case something goes wrong and you can keep it down. We tried to keep a dry space [i.e. no alcohol]. I'm sure it went on, it happens … but as long as it wasn't too public or getting too messy, what can you do? Having an open door does work, but you do need to secure it in a soft way, just for everybody's safety. For the building's safety. For people's safety.

As squatters, the volunteer crew had no more ownership over the building than the people coming to stay there, which meant they had no more *formal*

Figure 14 'Every squat counts' (TAA, 2018)
Source: Image by the author.

authority than anyone else to say who could or could not stay (although, this is not to say that hierarchies didn't exist). The reason it worked, however, was that everyone had a stake in keeping the space viable and, materially, there was a large amount of space available across the building, which meant people could find somewhere without encroaching too much on others:

> Over a three-week period ... you're talking hundreds of people ... I'd say one or two people had to be ejected, maximum. Which considering ... is nothing. And generally, when they sobered up and got themselves gathered, they came back, and that was ok. And in future they actually *became* the security! (laughs) Because they saw: 'Yeah they were right actually, I was a dick, fair enough.'

There were also other divisions in the space. The first floor was almost exclusively Roma and, chatting to a few people on the ground floor, there was some clear (sometimes racialised) resentment around a birthday party which had kept people awake the night before. I asked Yale whether there had been any racial tensions within the squat, but his take was that these divisions simply reflected people sticking with people they felt comfortable with:

There wasn't that much tension to be honest with you ... bizarrely. Because people thought it must kick off, but there was a great interaction between the different ... we were creating the right ambience around it ... an acceptable, tolerating thing.

For Yale, squats have some potential to be spaces of encounter, in which diverse communities can be created:

When you start living together you get a tight bond. And this is why we need to open up *more* buildings, so therefore we can get new crews developed. Having a 'crew' definitely does help facilitate the smooth running of the building. But it does have that reflection of society which does become 'hierarchical' in a way.

Sofia House demonstrated the possibility of property relations of inclusion and care, even if this was challenging at times. Yet the impending eviction and constant media scrutiny of the squat was a constant reminder of how the wider dominance of the ownership model would ultimately render this space precarious and temporary:

You *can* develop a sustainable community. You can develop somewhere where people can share skills. You can create life-changing spaces, believe it or not. But there are some negatives to squatting because of the nature of it. The perpetual moving leads to mental health issues ... Generally, you're not keeping a squat for more than three weeks. And that in itself creates problems because you're always ready to move ... It's great if you get a few weeks to maybe get your head down. But you're always on the move again ... which does suit some people. It suited me! I was alright with that lifestyle. But other people you could definitely see, with their mental health, that they needed that *stability*.

Yet, as a port in a storm, squatting can also be a quick and efficient way to open up wasted spaces, and Yale's take on the future role of squatting was defiantly optimistic:

I see squatting as a solution to the housing crisis ... it also gave me, myself, somewhere to live! And a base for setting up operations. I mean, that's where Streets Kitchen came out of ... we came out of the squatting movement. Because for me, squatting done properly is a solution to the housing crisis, and to community value. Giving space for marginalised groups to meet to do whatever they need to do.

1

These People Need Homes, These Homes Need People

Why are there people sleeping and dying outside vacant buildings? In 2014, Danny Dorling argued that 'the ultimate problem in recent decades has not been too little building, but growing inefficiency in our use of the housing stock that we have'.[1] Yet over a decade later, the Office for National Statistics estimates that there are currently 1.3 million truly vacant dwellings across England.[2] Meanwhile, even if we include the 8,442 people the government (under-)estimates to be sleeping rough across the country,[3] the 289,430 households that approached local authorities for housing support between 2022 and 2023,[4] and the estimated 100,000 people who are 'hidden homeless' (moving between squats, sofa-surfing, sheds and van-living, or trapped in abusive domestic situations to avoid sleeping rough) – this only comes to around 400,000. In England, there are enough vacant dwellings for every homeless person to have a second home.

Rough sleeping is the extreme end of housing precarity and crisis. Defined by exposure, it means that people must find or keep somewhere safe to sleep outside, maybe while coping with addiction or trauma; needing to be wary of passers-by, dealing with the weather and law enforcement, perhaps trying to negotiate a night on someone's sofa or a bus. But housing crisis also exists on different levels across society, including for those working every waking hour in poorly paid and unfulfilling jobs just to meet the unreasonable rents of a city like London, or those fighting to stop their social housing estate from being 'regenerated' (that is, the occupants being evicted, and the buildings demolished and replaced with unaffordable flats). To call it 'the' housing crisis is therefore misleading. Not only does 'crisis' mean different things to different people in different circumstances, it also suggests a momentary blip in an otherwise fair and just housing distribution. As Madden and Marcuse have pointed out, 'for the oppressed, housing is always in crisis'.[5] Instead of *the* housing crisis, we should instead refer to just 'housing crisis' as a visceral, personal, and material experience of property relations under the ownership model. The current situation is not a temporary problem. The housing system as it currently exists *is* crisis, because it creates and reproduces 'chaos, fear and disempowerment'[6] for millions. Housing crisis is the contemporary capitalist city functioning *normally* and homeless people sleeping outside of vacant homes illustrates the logic of this exclusionary system in action.

The very way 'home' is currently imagined through the lens of ownership – as something secure, defendable, as well as (ideally) owned and exchangeable – is implicated in a system that perpetuates home*lessness*. While someone might not be experiencing housing crisis, therefore, they are still 'very much part of the mechanism perpetuating it'.[7] Michele Lancione has argued that our idea of a 'normal' home actually *depends* 'on the expulsion of the other ... [as] the basis for the extraction of a sense of security, entitlement and belonging'.[8] Being 'homed' and being 'homeless', in other words, are treated as opposites, but this artificially covers over the way in which they are systematically connected as 'coherent expressions of a wider sphere founded upon a shared affective and political economy'.[9] The same system that promotes a (home) ownership model through the market is that which structurally excludes and violently denies.

In many cities, the perennial problem with housing is that 'the pursuit of profit ... is coming into conflict with its use for living'.[10] The issue is that the value of space is not being expressed in terms of its actual or potential use on the ground, but instead in terms of potential return on investment. In the minds of investors, policymakers, and property owners, the use of a space is often secondary to its value as an asset. A building or a plot of land becomes something which can be obtained, owned, flipped for profit, built into a 'nest egg' for selling upon retirement, and/or passing on to the next generation (in the context of a stripped social welfare system).[11] Price and need have become completely divorced. The economic value of a space instead reflects artificial demand which has been inflated by the creation of scarcity. Under this property system, the value of a space is not its use, but its alienability. The value of a building is not whether it is meeting a need for housing in a certain location, but its *potential* for profitable exchange on the market, leading to 'warehousing' behaviour (i.e. where an owner keeps a space empty or under-used, waiting for local scarcity to inflate demand and therefore value).

Asking the question 'who is London for?', Anna Minton points out that capital is being allowed to flow into 'every aspect of land, property and housing',[12] which means that 'exchange value ... has entirely broken the connection with its use value ... when it comes to housing, prices are failing to respond to the needs of most people'.[13] The only way to explain the frenetic building going on in London when there is widespread vacancy and homelessness, is to recognise that it is the wrong houses that are being built. As new buildings are designed and built in order to be immediately snapped up as second homes or Airbnb-style listings, existing buildings are simultaneously being demolished as part of regeneration schemes (despite the fact that retro-fitting existing empty buildings would be a much more sustainable approach in a climate emergency).[14] The creation of artificial scarcity and homelessness in London is driven by global capital and a neoliberal political system, underpinned by the ownership model of property:

> at the heart of the housing crisis are those theories that housing is best allocated by a market open to speculation ... shelter then becomes the cornerstone of the economy, the main sink of wealth and savings ... being made homeless, apparently, is the threat that drives the market ... homelessness is the stick, wealth is the carrot.[15]

And yet the neoliberal state has long been reluctant to 'provide low-cost, flexible housing to realistically meet the demands of the poorest and most vulnerable members of their communities' and seems 'more predisposed to commit their resources after the fact'.[16] As Jacobs has argued, 'in most instances, governments have sought to protect the value of property above many other concerns'.[17] At various levels – national, regional, local – authorities proactively facilitate the market to provide housing designed for *ownership*, while simultaneously shirking any social responsibilities towards non-owners.[18] The upshot is that any 'viable' solution to housing crisis becomes restricted to the ownership model. The automatic championing of home ownership aligns with constructions of what counts as good citizenship, or who is a good citizen, based upon 'rugged' self-sufficiency and conspicuous consumption'.[19] Of course, such 'rugged self-sufficiency' isn't a virtue attributed to squatters, and homelessness is seen more as a result of individual shortcomings than the inevitable outcome of a systematically exclusive and inequitable housing system.

Instead, we need an approach to housing crisis that starts *not* from prevailing systems of ownership but which instead recognises the 'radical politics of inhabitation arising from the embodied experiences of those currently defined as un-homed'.[20] By looking at home from the perspective of the margins, rather than from the perspective of the current system, which positions marginalised people as 'less', we can diversify our understanding of home beyond the ownership model. As Colin Ward argued, 'one shouldn't really make plans about housing but develop "an attitude" that "will enable millions of people to make their own plans"'.[21] Through occupation, grassroots organising, and squatting, there is the potential for flexible and inclusive spaces which can liberate the 'desire for a thousand different homes to emerge'.[22] Not all of these spaces will be sustainable, viable, or successful, but they can be more efficient and empowering than current political and economic policies around housing.

Squatting is an efficient way to turn wasted buildings into housing because, through bypassing the state and the market, it provides a direct route for accessing needed space. Squatting is a direct response to an exclusive and inefficient housing market that systematically fails to distribute property according to social need. But squats can also be a precarious and dangerous form of shelter and, despite being driven by an inclusive ethic, crews often have to navigate who may or may not be considered a 'legitimate' user of a space. Individual squatters and crews regularly face difficult decisions around the criteria for evicting others from a space. For some, the answer was simply to have an 'open-door' policy, leading to often chaotic and potentially harmful domestic situations. For others, the key was a tight crew of people you could trust and wanted to live alongside. For most, the practicalities of squatting meant adopting a flexible position somewhere in between, one which often changed from building to building.

RECYCLING THE EMPTIES

Asher picked up his beer, 'at the end of the day, they're resources. We recycle bottles, glass, cans ... and all that. But we don't recycle buildings? We should be!'

Sat in the corner of a vegan Thai restaurant on Kentish Town Road, we finally had a plate of food, but it had taken us quite a while to get here. Walking down Camden High Street, we stopped every few minutes to greet another person he knew. I say 'knew', but I quickly learn that few people in squatting know each other by their real name, with most people adopting a pseudonym and then the squat they are most associated with as their last name (leading to family names such as Rainbow, Cooltan, and Hive). Asher had been a squatter in London for a long time, involved in establishing community centres, housing campaigns, creating spaces to organise against war or austerity, and taking action on the global climate emergency. Well-connected, Asher often referred to himself as a 'networker' instead of an 'activist', and once joked he was 'the squatter directory of north London'. Despite a long and active role in various movements, however, when he first got involved, he was less motivated by the politics and more by the simple need to find somewhere to live. 'Mainly I got into squatting because it was a survival thing ... it was somewhere to go when I didn't have anywhere to go because I got homeless.'

As a teenager, he had been subletting from students in London and working 'some crappy office job'. However, when the students decided to leave the tenancy three months early, Asher lost his £400 deposit and suddenly found himself out on the streets:

I basically couldn't afford to get a deposit and get another place. Didn't have any savings kind of thing ... ended up on the streets for a while ... then basically bumped into some mates again who were squatting in King's Cross. So that was quite a lifesaver because I'd been kind of begging on the streets and just like ... hectic. So yeah, stayed with them for a while.

While in King's Cross, he had slept on the living room floor for a couple of months but found it difficult when other squatters would come into the communal area to party. He befriended a bicycle courier who was also living there, and they got hold of a copy of the *Squatters Handbook* before heading up to an estate to find an empty two-bedroom council flat:

The back window was open! Got in ... people upstairs took pity on us, two young lads needing somewhere to live, so they gave us the [door] combination. So, we had our first little two-bedroom flat squat. Really happy. We were there for about 4–5 months: drew on the walls, ate toast, go out and score some blim [marijuana] once a week ... you used to get so much more time with squatting in those days, especially if it was a council place. It took them a few weeks or months to realise you were there because they had 2,000 empty buildings.

For Asher, the fundamental point of squatting was to fulfil basic needs – 'to stay alive, to keep warm ... for most people the aim is to get out the fucking cold ... squatting is survival ... they've given it a bad name, but squatting could easily be called "sheltering"'. Back in the early 1990s, it was a way for him to get a roof, walls, windows, a door, and the possibility of heating, lighting, running water, as well as the privacy that he didn't find at King's Cross. However, it steadily became *more* than this:

You manage to reclaim your *time*. Suddenly you have 40 hours of your life back. I mean, I worked out at one point that I could carry on working … I was on £105–£110 a week. By the time I've paid rent, paid for travel, paid for food … I basically had a tenner and an eighth of hash left from my working for a week. And then I worked out if I was squatting … I actually had 40 hours of my life back … and I had like a quarter to smoke and £20! So, actually, I was better off reclaiming my time and doing what I wanted with it … a lot of people in squatting are very *very* skint and kind of live in that area of marginalised, vulnerable, hand to mouth … But to me, it was for many years an amazing opportunity to get into some incredible buildings of all shapes and sizes, and to organise for the environment. That's my main passion.

Over time, this passion led Asher to open spaces as community centres. Inspired by the Twyford Down anti-roads protests and the Rio Earth Summit in 1992, he was a founding member of the Rainbow Tribe, who set up Rainbow Centres across North London. It's at this point, he tells me, that squatting 'really became a space where it wasn't just about survival and living, it was about creating a space that other people could come into and use, where we could interact, where we could be reclaiming the commons':

We went and squatted the big old church up in Kentish Town. Probably one of the most famous Rainbow Centres. Got a deal off the Church of England. Had it for about two and a half years, packed it with events, parties, conferences, meetings, workshops, organised a lot of the road protest movement and Criminal Justice Act [protests] … and all sorts you know? We had a list of 20 different things you can do with an empty building: community centre, café, library, arts space, craft space, kids space, DIY, self-employed, market, bike repair, computer repair … whatever it was, you know?

Sean had a similar story in which his personal housing needs overlapped with his politics. Originally living with his sister, he moved back home when she died in 1987, but 'then that got stressful', so he decided to squat with a mate in Clapham:

It was a three-bedroomed flat, council flat. So went for it, yeah, I was 21 I think. And yeah, so I squatted there for about a year I think … Got nicked for breaking a squat for someone. What we did was break a wooden door and that was it, £50 fine, £50 costs. And just slowly got into the network of squatters you know ... ended up slowly sort of drifting towards Brixton ...

Managing to get some casual work as a decorator, Sean only made enough income to make ends meet because he wasn't paying rent: 'I couldn't believe that people worked just to live in a house (laughs) with not a lot else left ... which unfortunately is still the case I hear! (laughs).' There was a clear ethic which motivated him to squat, a set of principles which bled over from his housing precarity into a political position on housing crisis, and views on *how* empty spaces should be repurposed:

We were very much into keeping the house together, you know? Doing building work on it ... So, most of the time, the neighbours loved us because they were like 'well, our heating bill goes up when the houses are empty ... and also, we don't have any rats thanks to you lot'. I felt like we were sort of the mice that sort of clean up all the food that's left scattered, you know? Stitch up all the gaps in the society and you know... just *use*. I was proud of not charging the housing benefit. I didn't claim housing benefit when I was squatting ... 25 years up until six years ago that I'd been squatting: that'd be a hell of a lot of housing benefit if I wasn't working!'

Opening up empty spaces for housing was simultaneously about setting up spaces for communal living *and* making a political point about vacant buildings by deliberately 'doing them up' (repairing and upgrading the building in order to make it liveable):

As soon as we got in, we set up a communal kitchen. We'd get a fridge there and people went and skipped food ... [and] it'd be put in the middle and anyone who turned up it's like: 'look, there's couches. Get you a blanket if you want. Help yourself to food. if there's no milk, please fill it up ...' [you] just get that sort of project *together* ... I think most squats have a sort of front room with lots of couches and you get a sort of handful of regular mates that sort of ... I used to escape from my hostel for a couple of days and go and stay ... And you know I'd end up washing up, I'd end up, you know, doing artwork there, getting involved, people would go 'Oh, do you want a coffee?' and come back with stuff. I'd get fed. And yeah, it was like having a sort of family that I could just escape to and feel at home. And I was accepted, it was lovely.

The establishment of community within squats and the wider squatting scene was a central component, Sean argued, to the inherent politics of squatting, because it 'shows models of what's possible ... there's a lot of communal support that I think is missing out in society':

> I think when people are homeless you know they've got loads going on ... you've got to get your drugs, get your food, get sleep, get safe, get water for the dog or whatever ... [squatting] is having a free space where you can just help yourself ... just a bit of free space to express themselves and to get creative ... there's a lot of pleasure in shared effort and vision.

For Sean, creating these shared spaces was a political act because of the context of an inaccessible wider housing system. By setting up communal living spaces, the aim was to exist outside of the norms of the ownership model altogether – 'you know, it's not *my* house, it's *our* house', as he put it, giving examples of a 'family atmosphere' in some buildings where they didn't lock their rooms and allowed people to come in to get cigarettes or play someone else's record collection.

Occasionally, however, opening up such spaces by repairing long abandoned and neglected buildings and bodies presented specific challenges. Sean related to me an experience in one squat where he 'ended up having several really *really* violent nasty fights with this bloke', but 'actually ended up in hospital for three weeks ... with streptococcal malaria [meningitis] [from] trying to clean the drains'. It might have been housing crisis which led Sean to squat in the first place, but it was also a combination of problems stemming *from* housing crisis which ultimately led him to give up squatting:

> I've got really bad back injuries and sciatica and arthritis and porosis ... it's probably from sleeping rough and, you know, living in cold buildings ... [squatting] affected my health quite a lot ... [after the fight] I got pissed off and I just said 'that's it, fuck community living, all it takes it one idiot and that's it, messes the whole thing up' ... [but] one thing that really hit me was when the change in the rule [law] came about. Was literally within a week I lost contact with handfuls of people ... there was a good break-off from a lot of that community spirit. I think a lot of people got scattered and it's taken a bit of time for everyone to slowly find out where people are and get back into it.

For both Sean and Asher, living among people who had been socially marginalised, like themselves, also meant living alongside people with traumatic biographies, which sometimes manifested as 'difficult personalities', mental illness, and/or addiction. Inclusion was challenging, and occasionally violent, but this was also the point. While they both had experienced patches of rough sleeping and hidden homelessness, squatting meant not only a way to find housing, but also finding somewhere to belong, to free up time, to be part of something purposeful and meaningful. Housing crisis was something that they both had direct experience of, and which they had addressed directly through squatting (both in terms of practical need *and* politics). There was no distinction for them between 'political' and 'non-political' squats because, while it might be true that some squats could have a clear ideological bent, or align themselves with a campaign, simply recycling the empties in the context of an exclusionary and wasteful property system was political in itself.

ANOTHER LEVEL BEFORE THE STREET

Zara had a place to study philosophy, politics, and economics at Goldsmiths. However, not being from London, she hadn't anticipated the sheer cost of living in the capital:

> Student fees were nine grand a year. Rent was a lot. I didn't have any money and parents couldn't help. I was at uni full time ... a part-time job would have been difficult and wouldn't have got me enough money. I did try and go back to modelling, but I didn't get a lot of money out of that, and it actually takes a lot of time because there's a lot of unpaid work ... going to castings and that ... which clashed with classes. I don't know what else I could have done.

In a last-ditch attempt to finish her degree, Zara sofa-surfed with family friends, but she 'wasn't able to continue staying with them'. Briefly, she considered trying to rent a shared house, but found the idea of committing to a rental contract in the context of skyrocketing prices 'quite scary ... it's very formalised'. That's when she met some people at a protest:

> I just asked around basically. I ended up getting taken to one of the squats. It's *another level before the street*, isn't it? It's interesting, culturally and socially ... if you're lucky, you can meet a lot of people to make friends

with. There's networks. There's a lot of activist movements within it. I ended up dropping out of uni, but I was doing squatting instead, so I was *doing something*, you know?

Just at the point where Zara felt lost, on the brink of sinking into a world of insecure employment, housing precarity, and feelings of inadequacy after not completing her degree, squatting gave her purpose. The first crew she joined – the 'Autonomous Nation of Anarchist Libertarians' or 'ANAL' – were making a name for themselves, occupying high-profile vacant buildings in central London, including empty banks, corporate headquarters, and even an embassy, with the intention of turning these spaces into homeless shelters. The aim:

> was to show that there's empty buildings ... over winter, it was January/February, really cold ... But it was also just a 'fuck you!' as well. Especially when we [squatted] Admiralty Arch. A lot of homeless people came and lived with us ... but it was all just a piss-take as well.

I asked how the squats worked in practice with so many strangers coming to stay:

> There's so many problems. But we just sort of managed the problems by just being really chaotic ourselves. We were all moving [buildings] all the time and we didn't really care.

Here, the inherent precarity of squatting was turned into a (short-term) virtue. The open-door policy made the spaces chaotic and sometimes unsafe, yet the frequent and short-notice evictions also meant that the core of the group could reform again and again, 'burning through' each building when it became unsustainable. 'It did only last short term,' Zara explained, 'obviously people want to do things with their lives at some point ...'

ANAL was a fragile and temporary group of people experiencing various degrees of housing crisis, so it's perhaps unsurprising that rifts appeared. A group calling themselves Squatters and Homeless Autonomy (SHA) – 'we called them "Shit Housing Activists"', scoffed Zara – broke off, complaining that ANAL needed to party less and take the politics more seriously. However, this split seemed to upset a balance:

I stayed with [SHA] a bit. Ages later. And it was really depressing. Everyone seemed to have depression and they were saying they were doing more serious political stuff, but they ended up doing *nothing*. And then the rest of ANAL, without the most 'serious politically minded people', it just all got a bit silly.

This split demonstrates well both the porousness between different 'types' of squatting as well as the property relations that exist between the squatters themselves. Some went on to join the occupation at Sweets Way housing estate. Others reformed ANAL and pulled off their most high-profile squat in Belgravia in 2017:

That became a homeless shelter and that's when the new wave ANAL started. Which I thought was awful, basically, I really didn't like it. It was a *dictatorship*. No one was accountable really ... It was really gendered and along class and race lines as well. You often find that they'll say 'we have no hierarchy, it's horizontal' blah blah blah. And it's like: 'Ok, but the white man over there is obviously in charge and everyone knows it.' Often [however] the squats that *reflect* on it, and try and do something about it, are actually the *worse* squats ... People often call out hierarchies *to their own benefit*, not really to address the balance.

Belgravia seemed to lack the flexibility of the earlier ANAL squats where they were more willing to simply abandon a space if it became too messy. The public profile of this squat meant there was something at stake, so they made an active attempt to sustain the space by managing different uses and users within the building:

We basically had a pretty good open-door policy, to 'drag 'em in'. But we also had a really strict 'drag 'em out' policy. So, it was like: 'anyone can come in, but when you fuck up, we will drag you out' ... We didn't have meetings to decide. It was just kind of obvious. And most people would either get involved [in kicking someone out] or not ...

I asked what the criteria were for excluding someone from the squat. At what point was someone considered 'not alright' and therefore they needed to be 'dragged out'?

Erm … scaring the girls (laughs). Someone actually got kicked out for scaring the girls. And just being inappropriate. There was one guy who kicked himself out because he started a fire and then ran around with a shotgun. Turns out it wasn't a real shotgun in the end. But we thought it was. The armed police came and filled this whole squat.

Zara's experience of squatting had been a whirlwind and didn't bring her much in terms of long-term sustainability and security, however it did provide an immediate source of refuge and purpose at a time when she needed it the most. Early ANAL turned chaos to their advantage to maintain an open-door policy and avoid controlling or managing spaces as if they owned them. But, by her own account, it was also a piss-take: mocking a property system that would allow so many empty buildings to exist. The difficulty came when they tried to hold on to a space and were forced to make decisions around who could or could not use it. Not only did this create anti-democratic hierarchies – or a 'tyranny of structurelessness',[23] where some took advantage of the lack of formality to promote their own vision for the space – it also created unclear criteria for inclusion/exclusion, for which (potentially) no one was accountable.

Other crews aim to keep control of spaces by simply keeping their crew tight and familiar, as well as only squatting *smaller* buildings which they could physically defend from eviction if needed. In Heddy's case, this approach had given his crew some relative stability, because – in contrast to ANAL – they were in a better position to find temporary agreements with landlords if they kept their heads down and were less publicly chaotic.

I first met Heddy at Grow Heathrow (a squatted garden centre protesting a third runway at Heathrow Airport) where he performed some spoken-word poetry. After his set, we chatted over a six-pack of lukewarm Red Stripe, before he invited me up to his squat at Holloway Road. When I got there a few days later, he explained that they had managed to negotiate with the landlord that they could stay, as long as they kept the numbers low, didn't have any parties, and promised to leave the property when asked to:

He's had people in before that took the piss, basically. Did raves in there. Stripped the lead off the building and the ones surrounding it (because you can get out onto the roof) … Obviously not all squatters are ethical … Our crew has kicked quite a few people out of it who are, like, too intense or too messy or whatever.

This week, the landlord had finally given them notice, but was clearly worried that they wouldn't actually go and had offered to pay for a storage unit while they found somewhere else. However, the crew had gone out of their way to find a garage which was cheaper than the unit to save the landlord some money.

Heddy had originally experienced homelessness at 15 when he was kicked out of his family home. Being a minor, and having a 'diagnosed drug problem', initially he was able to find accommodation through the council. But after many years in the system, he eventually tried to move into the private rental sector:

> I ended up working full time in casinos. And I was working 40 hours a week to earn a grand a month to pay £500 a month in rent, which was like ... it's ridiculous. You're left with £125 a week for working full-time night shifts ... like slaving as well. £125 a week barely even covers my weed! (laughs) Which just isn't fair really, I don't think. You've got to work 40 hours a week to have a lack of financial control ...

In direct comparison to private renting, squatting offered a different prospect:

> I've lived in three places in the last two years and they've been pretty nice comfortable places ... I can get by without having any money because I smoke cigarettes off of the floor (which I know is pretty bad, but you can do that). And I can get my food from bins and I don't have to pay any rent. And that's pretty much all of your life main expenses covered. And then I've got all of my time to then be able to do whatever it is that I want to do with my time!

I was given a tour of the squat. A former doctor's clinic, the building was well set up for living in. Each examination room had been repurposed as a bedroom, while the old waiting room and staff kitchen were easily repurposed into a communal living area. There were even multiple toilets (although they had been struggling to get one to flush properly).

Being able to hang on to spaces for a sustained length of time meant that squatting was actually *less* precarious than Heddy's experience in hostels or the private rental sector. It also gave him more time to be involved in worthwhile activities, rather than simply working to meet the cost of living:

When I was working full time and I wanted to get involved with stuff ... I had to try and fit that around the 40 hours a week that I was working. And, like, I used to want to go out and feed homeless people and stuff. And I did do it sometimes, like, not as efficiently as I wanted to, but I'd go skipping and then go round and, like, leave food with the homeless people and stuff.

Once he had become involved in squatting, more opportunities came up to be involved in political campaigns surrounding housing crisis as well. One particularly remarkable occupation Heddy told me about was the time they squatted the headquarters of the property guardian company, Camelot:

Yeah, that was a big thing at CamaSquat ... because CamaSquat was initially a protest squat and nothing else. There was three of us opened it and we all had somewhere else to live. We were all doing it purely out of protest: to get it in the newspaper and to raise the conversation about the housing crisis ...

This was a direct protest against property guardian companies. These 'anti-squat' businesses, which have actively lobbied for the criminalisation of squatting, sell their services to owners of vacant properties, while taking advantage of people in situations of housing precarity. 'Guardians' are moved into the vacant properties but have no tenancy rights and can be evicted at a moment's notice, and yet they are contractually obliged to stay and secure the property for prolonged periods of time. For Heddy, the ironic joy of this occupation came from both the material conversion of offices into living space and that they were able to bring publicity to the issue:

CamaSquat was awesome. Like there was loads of problems there, but it was awesome (laughs). I don't know what we achieved in the two months we were actually there, really. But it was good because we got into the newspaper ... I think it created a lot of motivation at the scene ... Especially because the building was so nice as well. It had hot running showers, they had a big cooker in there with six hobs on it, fridges and freezers and a brand-new washing machine ... It was properly kitted out. And then plug sockets in the floor everywhere for where they put the tables in the office obviously ...

Similar to Zara's experience, the occupation became difficult when their protest against housing precarity was met with the consequences of housing precarity – when strangers in need of shelter began to approach the crew asking to stay in the building:

> There's a weird line of ... do we help these people? Or do we just tell them: 'Unless you want to be an activist, we can't help you?' We ended up helping them anyway, obviously, like, you can't just kick them out for not being an 'activist'. But we then try and encourage them to become more involved, try and explain to them ways that they can be involved ... Which is quite hard ... Some people did end up having to move out because they were so uninvolved with it ... Semi 'chose to go' and semi 'forced out', but like we would never have evicted anybody ... we would always make sure that someone's got somewhere to go before you tell them: 'You've got to leave.' Some people worked there as well ... go out to work, come back, and go out to work and come back. And we just weren't up for that, basically. We're not facilitating a place for people to work full time and live.

Both Zara's and Heddy's stories demonstrate that there is a difficult balance between making a political statement on empty homes/homeless people, yet keeping the occupation a viable space. Seemingly identifying more as an 'activist-squatter' at CamaSquat, Heddy might be classed as a 'non-activist' squatter back at Holloway Road. The different buildings were occupied for different purposes, no doubt, but this demonstrates the crossover of living and campaigning when in a housing crisis. Both directly grappled with questions of who could use the space. They couldn't really stop anyone from coming to stay there, if they were truly making a point about housing precarity. Yet, at the same time, how could they hope to hold on to the space if it descended into the chaos experienced by ANAL?

THE PRECARITY OF SQUATTING

It is important not to romanticise squatting, particularly in the context of intense stigmatisation and criminalisation. Squatters are forced to navigate the restrictive social norms of what property is, how it should be used and by whom, and this has rendered it an extremely insecure and precarious route to finding space, even before you take into account the likely poor condition of vacant buildings.

When I first met Dax, he was living in a converted ambulance around the backstreets of Brixton, constantly on the move to avoid parking penalties. He explained that squatting had become much more difficult since 2012, and the rise of property guardianships meant that a practice which was 'already very small [has] become next to nothing in most cities'. He speculated that some people who had squatted in the past, or who might have tried squatting in the present, were now turning to alternatives such as camper vans, converted trucks, or boat-living, but that even these were near-impossible for those at the extreme end of housing crisis.

Squatting was the only way Dax could have moved to London when he was 17. But while living and working in Brixton, he also got interested in the political and cultural sides of the scene, getting involved in the Cool Tan Arts centre and the campaign against the Criminal Justice Bill in the early 1990s. 'I was interested in what was going on,' he told me in a matter-of-fact way, 'and wanted to find out about the kind of alternative scene ... see whether I could get involved.'

Sometimes, Dax would park in a friend's yard while he worked shifts at Brixton market. A skilled and passionate chef, Dax often had to move from city to city to find work in a notoriously insecure and often poorly paid industry. Before being able to save up and afford his van, his only options were renting somewhere cheap and poor quality or finding a squat to join: 'I didn't really have security in terms of employment and I was a bit worried about putting money down for a deposit if I didn't know how long I would be able to hold down a tenancy.' Dax used squatting to stay mobile and maintain flexibility in finding work, as it allowed him to more easily shift locations. As Lynn Owens has argued, squatting can be as much about being mobile as staying put, producing new ways of relating and opportunities for solidarity, by multiplying contact points and facilitating a free flow of information. In other words, 'moorings make mobility possible ... they act as enablers'[24] and 'combine the demand to stay with the freedom to leave'.[25]

Along with finding this flexibility through squatting, however, comes precarity. On New Year's Eve 1997, Dax returned to the building he had been squatting to find Sitex sheeting on the windows and doors, with all his belongings inside:

> And yeah, had like a few days being *properly* homeless. Like, you know, just sleeping in the basement stairwell of a block of something like that ... just through word of mouth, a few people I knew who were squatting

in Clapham North ... went and knocked on the door and asked if I could stay with them, sometimes you get lucky that way.

Dax had clearly built up a lot of experience and knowledge over many years of having to hustle to find spaces to stay, and had stories both of being turned away by squatters who 'were worried about protecting their own space', as well as having to 'crack' squats without much back-up:

> Getting into all sorts of sticky situations. Breaking somewhere with a friend ... and then like half an hour later some thugs coming through the back door to chase us out with bats ... Being stuck up on an icy roof first thing in the morning: I had to stay there spread-eagled being invisible for 20 minutes until they waited for a clear window and came back, put the ladder back on. You have to ease yourself down to the edge of the roof and make a leap of faith of dangling one leg off the edge of the roof onto the ladder and then coming back down. Luckily at the time, I actually worked in the solar energy industry, so being on roofs wasn't something I was completely unfamiliar with ... but usually with scaffolding!

While living in Bristol, Dax described an opportunity he had to negotiate with the property-owner to keep using the premises:

> I'd come to the end of my tether with trying to squat buildings ... I mean it's hard enough just like living with people normally, let alone with all the stresses of squatting. And being evicted ... So, I just found an empty lot round the back of a burnt-out building, and I built a den there ... the place was sold off for auction and the new owner, once he found out there was some weirdo camping in the yard, he just left me be ... it was almost like having free security on site for him.

When I caught up with Dax a year later, he had been to France and Spain in his van, before moving up to Sheffield and living at a roadside camp with New Age travellers while working in a kitchen. He told me he was leaving. The situation at the site had become increasingly difficult, including one death from a drug overdose and increasing pressure from the council for them to leave. His plan was to save enough money to fix his van, before travelling down to find festival catering work over the summer (he'd already arranged work at Glastonbury Festival). It's stories such as Dax's which highlight both the diverse and overlapping reasons why people squat as well as the potential precarity, danger, and insecurity it entails.

Many of the squatters I spoke to had experience of grappling with what they perceived to be this Janus-faced nature of squatting, which had led them to become disillusioned with the practice entirely. Ugo and I were sat outside a café in Soho, trying to conduct an interview, but were repeatedly interrupted by people asking for money. Ugo made a sweeping claim that squatting was not seen as an option by many rough sleepers and, to prove his point, he asked the next person who came up to us if they would ever consider squatting. Without hesitation they said 'No', laughed, and walked away. 'Street homeless people don't squat,' Ugo argued, 'they doss in places, but they very *very* rarely pitch up ... they avoid situations where they are likely to be confronted by landlords.'

Once again, the wider context of squatting which places rough sleepers as illegitimate users of (even vacant) spaces means it becomes a dangerous and potentially violent option, even when compared with the street. Being in a building can leave you potentially trapped. But the fact that the buildings are often long abandoned can also present other difficulties. 'The reality is, that squatting is fucking fucking hard ... even if you're good at it, it's fucking hard.' Ugo gave me a pretty grim example:

In the property we occupied in Balham ... I mean, you have to get seriously good with your DIY skills, [it's] where I got all of my DIY skills, otherwise you have to contend with things like 'faecal rain'. Do you know what faecal rain is? When you have a toilet on the second floor that leaks onto the first floor... fucking unpleasant. You know, you've got to fix this shit. It's not for the faint-hearted because the properties that you inhabit are by and large really derelict. You have pest problems. You have asbestos. You have fungus. You have black mould. You have faecal rain ... and then also there's the community of people that you live with ... when you're starting out squatting you can be living with *anybody* and I did. I lived with heroin and crack cocaine addicts. I'd come back after work to find my room all I had left was a mattress.

Across a ten-year period, Ugo tells me, he squatted at least 36 different buildings, before deciding to set up his own business: negotiating with vacant property owners for 'meanwhile' leases on their buildings. Having started squatting in 2001, he found that the stigmatising campaign in the months before criminalisation in 2012, as well as the rise in property development and property guardians in London at that time, had a 'noticeable impact on our ability to find empty buildings'. However, he also hinted that the constant insecurity of squatting had left him burnt out:

It's a very *very* transient life ... actually, by the end of it, my mental health was pretty bad actually. I actually had to see a therapist! (laughs) The stress of the life ... in my case it really took a toll. The constant stress. We were lucky ... we were in one place for four years ... another place two years and in another place six months, eight months. But in many of the places in between we were there for weeks. Never knowing whether the landlord's going to break in, never knowing when that fucking court order's going to come through the door, never being able to settle ... Everything has a price and squatting has a price. The price you pay for living rent-free is the price you pay in security. The price of building your home up from scratch – replumbing, redecorating, rewiring – with constant uncertainty of never knowing when you're going to be out.

And yet, despite the insecurity and the difficulties of squatting, Ugo argued that 'squatting is, in my opinion, an absolute social necessity'. For Ugo, 'empty buildings translate into direct opportunity'. This might be on a very personal level in terms of finding belonging and 'security' in a community (even if squatting itself has been made incredibly insecure). Squatting provided much-needed spaces where social connections and mutual support can happen, especially for marginalised communities:

One of the leading mental health concerns in the UK is social isolation ... it's experienced by vulnerable people. Whether they be people who are ostracised by their families or for their political beliefs or the fact that they may be gay or any other variety of reasons. It may be people who are mentally unwell (and there are a lot of those in the squatting community). It gave them a sense of belonging ... so much of that has gone thanks to the criminalisation of squatting.

It gave a sanctuary to thousands and thousands of vulnerable people. It gave a community to people who desperately needed a community. And it served as a catalyst to help some extraordinary talent shape our [London's] identity as a cultural destination ... It is such a vitally important thing to help people get ideas off the ground. Sometimes all you need when you are struggling to pay your rent and you're struggling to get some perspective or you're struggling to learn about yourself ... sometimes what you really need is a place you can step back and enjoy some autonomy. And that's what squatting gave us.

A SOLUTION FOR HOUSING CRISIS?

Many who recognise the need for squatting nevertheless argue that it is no longer a viable solution to housing crisis (if indeed it ever was). They emphasise that the reality of squatting today is constant precarity, meaning that squats struggle to provide the stability, security, or longevity that we might associate with a 'home', instead exposing already vulnerable groups of people to further marginalisation.

An employee of one of London's big homelessness charities agreed to an interview with me, but was initially very nervous about taking part, and only agreed on the condition of strict anonymity both for herself and her organisation. Her views on squatting were compassionate, yet also quite narrow, and she was particularly vocal that it could never be a viable response to housing crisis:

Desperation and destitution, I think, is why people turn to squatting … The aim of squatting is, of course, to remove people from street homelessness. Of course it is. Even in some instances, it's to create wellbeing centres, to create places that are a hub for communities … that's the ideal beautiful rainbow-covered version of what squatting is. What squatting is, in reality, is homelessness. And it is living without having your rights addressed. You don't have a tenancy in your name, so therefore if you were to then present to a local council and say 'Hi, I've been living here for five years or two years … you now have a duty of care to me.' They'll say, 'Where's your proof, buddy?'

By living informally and under the radar, one of the problems she saw with squatting was the inability to prove a 'local connection' when applying for housing support from the local authority (who prioritise the distribution of housing stock to those who have been living in the area). This was a practical argument that homeless people should register and engage with the system to access programmes and resources made available to them. While recognising that some squats created spaces of solidarity, her counter-argument was that this was a naïve or overly romantic idea of squatting. In practice, she argued, squatting is a bleak and last-ditch option for people who have little other choice:

In an ideal situation, the squatting movement will solve homelessness. In the pragmatic reality of what squatting is, unfortunately, I don't think it will. If you're fortunate enough to be in a small or large squatting community that really look out for each other, and really take care of each other's wellbeing (be it mental, physical, societal, emotional, however ...) then lucky you. If, however, that squat is ... the colloquial term, a 'trap den' ... whereby the dealer lives in the squat with the addicts and nobody leaves, then that's the other really ugly side of the movement, where people are abused and people experience domestic violence constantly. And nobody knows about it because they don't have a domicile to connect the violence to. So that's a darkness to it as well ... I love the idea of removing people off the streets, of course, that's part of what I do. But it has to be safe and it has to look at people's wellbeing as the paramount [aim] of the movement.

Perhaps coming from a charity background meant that this interviewee only encountered the hardest examples of squatting. She certainly picked up on some of the critiques of squatting made by others, such as questioning the available resources. However, there is no consideration here that squats might act as a source of solidarity and support for those who have been on the receiving end of the violent consequences of the current housing system.

For her, new policy and legislation was part of the answer and a better response than grassroots approaches to housing:

With the new Homeless[ness] Reduction Act [2017] ... this is really important that people are able to document where they've been living because that's what gets councils to help you. And if we constantly provide interim camp-bed solutions for people, then we're not attacking the root cause of the problem, which is the government are not housing people. And so, if we give spaces for people to stay that are illegal, the government still don't have to deal with the problem ... it displaces the problem.

From her professional experience, 'a secure tenancy is what is needed'. This would allow the homeless to vote ('you know, you've got all of these squatters and none of them can actually vote, so the only people that can have an opinion are landlords!'), as well as a GP and dental care. In squats, she recognised some useful aspects, such as being able to save money towards a deposit on a flat in the private rental sector, or simply the ability 'to be constructing something and creating a home, of course, everybody wants a home'. But squatting, she argued, undermined this in the long run:

If you are unfortunate to keep picking the wrong vacant buildings … you know, some people get lucky, and they're like: 'Do you know what? I've squatted this building for five years, the landlord's so wealthy he's got no idea that I'm here, lucky me' or 'The council have completely forgotten about this building for so long that I've just been here for a long, long time.' I don't think that's the majority. I think that for the majority of people, is a cyclical thing … move on and move on and move on, which is not good for you. Everybody needs a base, even if it's just somewhere to go from and come back to every so often.

Others that I spoke to, especially those who had direct experience of squatting with diverse crews across multiple buildings and periods of time, also recognised the problems raised by this housing charity worker, but came to different conclusions. Luis, for example, had been heavily involved at Sofia House and with Streets Kitchen in general. He had first started squatting 'up North' when he was younger because he was homeless:

So, I squatted a place myself, with a couple of friends. And yeah, we used it for a couple of months, we kept it in good conditions like, you know what I mean. Then we moved out once we'd used it for an address and everything so that we could get ourselves back on our feet.

Later he'd moved to London – I got the impression that Luis had been squatting in the city for quite a long time – more recently coming across Streets Kitchen and getting involved:

I think Yale's ideal of squatting is sort of my ideal of squatting as well anyway, you know what I mean? It's sort of how it should be done … with what they did with Sofia House. It became London's biggest homeless shelter within a week, in a time when it was snowing and it was minus outside and people were dying … it was on the news. People were dying in the streets and stuff and they got doctors in that place and everything. People went to hospital with pneumonia. Imagine if them people would have stopped outside that night in the minus conditions in the snow? They'd have been dead. That place really changed some people's lives in that week.

It was the direct action of Sofia House that appealed to Luis much more than squats which labelled themselves as 'political' which he saw as potentially problematic:

If you're saying your building's political [shakes his head] you know what I mean? You can't be shutting people out. You become non-political right there, mate! You become just like the few at the top who have got big [empty] buildings and are fucking letting people sleep on the streets.

No one I spoke to was under the impression that Sofia House was free of problems. Part of the reason, Luis suggested, was that it was just a 'large empty space mainly, it wasn't really separate rooms or anything', but what he valued was that, despite the challenges, 'they made it work, they made it work and people lived there and they got on alright (laughs)'.

What struck me about Luis' framing of Sofia House was his acceptance that it was, as a shelter with an open-door policy, chaotic at times. Yet the fact that it somehow still held together just long enough to get through the deadly weather front outside was a success in itself. Each person that came through the door wasn't treated as a potential threat to the viability of the space because they only had to keep things going for a limited amount of time. This meant that the precarity of the space, in a twisted sort of way, actually allowed for the empowerment of people who stayed there, because they didn't have to worry about being 'political enough' or 'sober enough' or 'vulnerable enough' to justify their use of the space:

One thing I've learnt working with Streets Kitchen and everything is that people from all walks of life and from all sorts of cultures end up on the streets for all sorts of reasons, you know what I mean? There's so many reasons and it can happen so easily in this country to be honest. You'd lose your job and then all of a sudden you've got nowhere to live. Most people aren't tight with their families in Britain either ... we've lost the fucking community aspect of it as well ... It's that community aspect.

Because it had been such a high-profile action, many of the squatters I met in 2018 referred to Sofia House in order to position themselves on these subjects. Oz, for instance, pointed to the occupation as an example of what squatting could do to address housing crisis, but also as demonstrating some of the limits of squatters housing people:

A lot of the people at Sofia House would squat if they could, but a lot of people also have a lot of issues that are not something that can be dealt with by a squat community. They're unequipped for it. It would be great if we were, but we're not. And you know, the idea of just simply housing people can lead to problems for people who are of a different state of mind, who, for them to inhabit the same space as someone else, can lead to dangerous situations.

However, for Oz, while this might mean that squatting was not a viable solution in the long run, it could still provide a much-needed immediate space for people to get support, find respite, and the time to regather themselves:

> I think it's more important that we provide the facilities for people to figure out what is best for them, in Sofia House, rather than talking about opening up a new building. Just simply opening buildings up for people isn't a long-term solution at all. Squatting itself is not a long-term solution, it's a short-term solution to a long-term problem. That's why we did Sofia House ... it was an emergency. People were literally at risk of dying on the street. People died in all sorts of other cities. There were 150 at least people coming through there. It made a point. It made a statement.

Squatting can be a double-edged sword. While it can be a direct way to address homelessness – whether to avoid rough sleeping, overstaying with friends and family, or the poor-quality end of the private rental sector – it is also fraught with the dangers of entering abandoned buildings (asbestos, leaks, faulty wiring, poor sanitation, broken glass, needles and detritus, as well as the physical act of getting in). The precarity and insecurity of eviction has worsened the more squatting has been criminalised and there is always a vulnerability to possible violence, whether from landlords staging illegal evictions (like the thugs with baseball bats kicking out Dax) or sometimes from fellow squatters (for instance, those with substance abuse or mental health issues, and even sexual abuse or rape). The risk of these factors varies from building to building and from crew to crew, but this highlights the contradiction that, while squatting can offer security and safety from homelessness and housing precarity, it can simultaneously be precisely the opposite. Sometimes, forming a crew and squatting a building is a gamble.

A SAFETY NET BELOW THE SAFETY NET

The coexistence of peopleless homes and homeless people is the direct consequence of a property system that prioritises the legal and moral right of (en)titled owners over any social responsibility to put vacant spaces to use. The societal value of space is expressed in terms of price, exchange, and profit, while any consideration of social purpose or utility is sidelined. Championing and defending ownership title allows an asset to be alienated from the context where it is located, denying any opportunity for negotiation or conflict on the ground. Instead, squats are providing informal spaces where that negotiation can take place (if only momentarily, before the vacant space is then returned to its 'proper place' in the market). In this way, even those squatters who consider themselves lucky when they find a landlord that is willing to let them stay temporarily, still find that they are *illegitimate* users of the space when the owner reasserts their recognised right to exclude them. Those who need space, but fall outside the ownership model of legitimacy, are demonised, stigmatised, and *weaponised* as threats, which justifies greater criminalisation and state intervention. Despite using their liberated time outside of the wage–rent vortex to pursue often benevolent or at least socially reproductive and pro-community tasks, squatters are instead held up as an example of what it looks like *not* to be a citizen, *not* to belong or to be part of the city.

It was perhaps no coincidence that the last wave of criminalisation targeting squatting across Europe happened in the wake of the 2008 financial crash. Not only did this 'crisis' sharpen systems of dispossession, dislocation, foreclosure, substandard or expensive housing; but it also simultaneously created vacancies. As Vasudevan puts it:

> it is, in this context, not hard to see the new wave of anti-squatting legislation as an attempt to protect the ongoing commodification of housing at a moment when many people are looking to alternatives that reassert the cultural, social and political value of housing as a universal necessity and as a source of social transformation ... [new laws] seek to uphold the sanctity of private property and defend the interests of 'hard-working homeowners' against squatters.[26]

From the early 2000s onwards, Manjikian traces a discernible shift in the way squatting has been framed. Studying political and media discourse across the UK, France, Denmark and the Netherlands – all of which introduced new anti-squatting legislation just after the 2007/8 financial crash – she argues that squatting moved from being seen as a domestic 'nuisance', which was occasionally treated with sympathy, or at least understanding, in the context of housing crisis, to something that was 'constructed as a threat to the state'.[27]

In these circumstances, any moral arguments around the utility of squats, let alone compassionate recognition of the causes of squatting in the first place, were swept aside by fearful, demonising and stigmatising rhetoric. Squatting came to be seen not as an outcome of housing crisis or the prevailing property system, but as 'a threat to national identity and national security',[28] demonstrating the way in which housing policies can be used to legitimise state authority, allowing the authorities to step in on the grounds of ensuring 'the safety and security of residents and their homes as well ... the state is seen as responsible for the security being provided at all these levels'.[29]

Within this context, squatting has become an even more dangerous and hazardous way to access space. In this chapter, we have seen that most squatters first occupied a building because they needed somewhere to live. More than a roof, they were looking for a *home*, yet their aims often varied, depending on the building, the crew, and the particular circumstances of each particular squat. There are plenty of examples where the stress of squatting has exacerbated some of the side-effects of marginalisation – mental and physical illness, addiction, or simply difficult personalities. The constant risk of intimidation or even violence from landlords, neighbours, police, and bailiffs; the ongoing insecurity given the constant possibility of eviction after having invested your sweat and soul into repairing a building and perhaps even establishing a sense of domesticity; the risk that the next building will be in a worse state than this one, having been neglected and left empty by a wasteful and inefficient economic system – the circumstances in which squatting takes place today means that it isn't always a straightforward or viable solution to housing crisis for everyone.

And yet, despite making squatting more difficult, it is these circumstances that makes it so crucial for many. As Yale put it to me, 'squatting is not the right solution, it's not the end solution, but it's the immediate solution'. While the first crew or squatted space someone joins might be particularly chaotic because of their open-door policy, the ties and solidarities which can emerge from these networks can come to resemble something like a family. Some squats might decide to embrace the chaos and quickly burn out, other tight-knit groups look for spaces which are more precisely suitable for their needs and desires, creating spaces which can sustain communities and free time. Other crews sit precariously between these two poles, but what all squatting represents is a very clear embodiment of the unjust politics and economics of vacancy. Whether this is made explicit or not, squatters are driven, in principle, to 'recycle the empties', albeit for a diversity of reasons.

For some, it is the safety net below the (threadbare) safety net of a welfare system wracked by austerity and the retreat of the neoliberal state. But squats are just as fraught as any other domestic spaces, in that they simultaneously embody security and insecurity. On the one hand, we might think of a home as providing 'ontological security', a term originally coined by psychologist R.D. Laing, but which has become a popular way to characterise what we mean by 'home'. Atkinson and Jacobs describe ontological security as 'the human need for assurances in the predictability of daily social life and our deep need for a sense that the world around us is stable and can offer a sense of continuity',[30] while Maddan and Marcuse emphasise 'the sense that the stability of the world can be taken for granted ... the emotional foundation that allows us to feel at ease in our environment and at home in our housing ... it presupposes stable access to dwelling space that is under the resident's own control'.[31] But while this is perhaps what we imagine or aspire to when we think of a 'home', we also know that the home is fraught for many:

> The home is one of the primary sites of physical violence and a place where long-running, deep, psychic injuries occur, often focused around gender relations and household conflict ... although the private home is cultur-ally positioned as a place of intrinsic social goodness, shelter, and personal autonomy, it is simultaneously the locus of widely shared emotions – fear, increasing social precariousness, and ... ontological insecurity – the sense that the very world around us is unpredictable and a threat.[32]

But homes are not simply sanctuaries that may or may not provide ontologi-cal security. They are part of a wider patriarchal and heteronormative society of familial relations; they are part of a market which designs and exchanges buildings for profitability rather than use; they are part of an unequal dis-tribution of resources along the lines of race, ethnicity, and class. For many who default on their mortgages or rent payments, or who find themselves criminalised simply for trying to find a space to live (including squatters, roadside Gypsy-Travellers, rough sleepers, asylum seekers ...), home can easily and very quickly be rendered an insecure space. After all, eviction for anyone, whether they were always considered illegitimate or have recently become an illegitimate user of a space, 'is the violent assertion of the rights of property owners over the needs of inhabitants'.[33]

The View from Denmark Hill

Figure 15   Imagine this as a window (Denmark Hill, 2018)
Source: Photo by a participant.

Wanda had taken a photo of a sheet of Sitex, bent upwards to let light in through the window. 'You can just transform the whole place!' her eyes gleamed, 'Instead of it looking haunted and abandoned, it could be *thriving*! All that sheeting has come off now. So, it looks less "squatty" and more inviting for the community ... The front's been cleaned up a lot.' Located down a leafy road of large, detached houses on Denmark Hill, keeping up appearances was important for maintaining a good relationship with the neighbours. 'I've always loved the area,' said Wanda, 'but felt very uncomfortable because of the looks I get from people':

> Posters were put up on every tree in the area for a community event ... when we went to it, it was really uninviting. Hostile. We felt like we needed to leave straight away ... I've got the most degrading looks I've ever got in my life just by standing outside the corner shop.

Figure 16   The original squatter (Denmark Hill, 2018)
Source: Photo by a participant.

The squat itself was a former nursing home. Wanda had been living there for a while and was trying to create some community engagement with the space, but was finding it difficult to organise support from a constantly rotating crew. Out the back, she wanted to open up the garden and small wooded area to the public which, according to rumour, was the location of the legendary 'Camber Well' and its healing waters. Through the trees at the back, we could see the glistening towers of the City of London and the Shard.

As we went back into the house, we passed a ginger cat sleeping on a chair in the hallway: 'He is the original squatter,' Wanda explained:

> I think you always need cats in squats because of the mice and rat situation. It helps things out. Last night we didn't sleep and it's a problem. When you start to hear rats running around, or mice or whatever they are, it takes away that homely feeling that you've created a space. And it doesn't matter how clean it is, it starts to take away the idea of it being clean, safe … safe to sleep in, safe to leave your food in.

Wanda had initially turned to squatting because she was back living with her parents for a third time. 'It just felt like I couldn't manage,' she recalled:

Figure 17   The City of London (from Denmark Hill, 2018)
Source : Photo by the author.

> The wage I was receiving from work and the amount I needed to spend
> to stay healthy ... the amount of *time* I needed to recuperate ... Renting
> didn't allow me to explore different types of jobs, and hobbies, and
> projects ... because there's always that fear of not being able to pay and
> being on the streets.

Compared to some of the squatters I had met, Wanda was relatively fortunate to have a family to fall back on. But she resented being trapped in a
wage–rent vortex just so she could afford to move out and still stay in the
city she called home. Squatting was her answer:

> It opens up free time and less stress. People can start remembering what
> their skills are and their passions are and purpose is. I think it's a door for
> these things ... personally, I used to feel like I just got too overwhelmed
> by the pressures of everyday working ... not have enough time to think
> of who I am, what I like doing, how I can help the world ... what's actually
> *going on* in the world, even.

Wanda was environmentally minded and experimented with propagation,
moss, and mycelium. She had been inspired by Grow Heathrow as a com-

Figure 18 A Camberwell fox (Denmark Hill, 2018)
Source: Photo by the author.

munity that emphasised the importance of living sustainably, although some iterations of the squat were better at supporting that vision than others:

> Grow Heathrow got me into it [squatting]. Just seeing how various people from different backgrounds can come together and create a community. It works, really. There's always going to be issues, but I'm sure it's the same in paid accommodation. Everyone has conflicts. But when [squats] don't work, I start to feel like depression in coming on, anxiety, even panic attacks ... [I start] asking 'what's the next move' and getting stuck in sticky situations.

When a squat breaks down, as with any family or community, the situation can be unbearable. Personalities clash. Privileges associated with masculinity, hetero-/cis- sexuality, whiteness, and class position can intersect in ways that create unaccountable hierarchies within the space.

Wanda, as one of only two women at Denmark Hill, felt that much of the domestic labour of maintaining a space where they could live comfortably and care for one another, fell on her shoulders:

Figure 19 'Anarchy is order so keep it clean!
Self-organise this kitchen' (Denmark Hill, 2018)
Source: Photo by the author.

I remember when we first moved in … it was expected that I would clean the kitchen everyday after food, but I was also helping to make food. Yeah, guys in general don't like to do the washing up or cleaning the surfaces in the kitchen or whatever. It gets a bit frustrating. I just stopped doing it. It was brought up in a meeting … that everybody needs to take responsibility to clean up after themselves … but depending on how much of a rush you're in, how high you are, how tired you are: it doesn't always happen.

The kitchen can be a microcosm of the overall viability of a living space. As well as being essential in terms of those in the building staying fed and healthy, communal meals also act as social glue, holding people together. Wanda told me that, while 'she didn't really mind' taking on the extra workload, she had decided it was best to stop stressing about it for her own wellbeing, especially after recently having a particularly rough time 'addressing resurfaced traumas'. But with the breakdown of the kitchen came a loss of communal care and mutual solidarity:

> In the end, we regressed into our room and we keep food in the room. When I stopped using the kitchen, the whole community broke down in a way. If I wasn't around to help with peeling, chopping, cooking, and cleaning afterwards, it just wasn't happening. But it just seemed like when I decided *not* to do that, it was my fault the community broke down. No one was having communal once-a-day meals together, discussing things.

While some of the more reflexive male squatters recognised what was going on and attempted to step up, they simply didn't experience the gendered structure of the space in the same way as Wanda, who began to feel personally responsible that the community within the building had collapsed:

> I think it was a lack of bonding, a lack of communication, feeling uncomfortable because we hadn't spent enough time ... We go to an M&S [supermarket] skip and get lots of food, but we also find really nice plants and flowers, mainly flowers and roses. So, when I had too much, I thought I might as well share them out around the house. I started putting them in bathrooms, in the hallways, in each room ... I duplicated my spider-plant [and] I put a pot outside each person's door ... It's nothing much, but just *something* to tie us closer. There was no cords between us.

Property divisions within the space began to be expressed materially, as individuals isolated themselves in rooms, or even attempted to make ownership claims over how certain space should or should not be used:

> The whole corridor: I just don't want to go near and it's literally right outside our bedroom. Because of a guy living here who is possessive over this kitchen and doesn't want anyone else using it because he was the one that 'cleaned it up the most' ... even though I helped him clean it. He gets annoyed. I still go in there when I have to ... even though I don't want to just because of him. He will slam his bedroom door shut when I go in there. It's just a ridiculous situation.

Wanda was quick to add, however, that many of the people who had moved into the squat were themselves dealing with trauma and the challenges of marginality, so she was quite sympathetic to the idea that not everyone might be ready to live communally, let alone participate in a public-facing

Figure 20 The corridor (Denmark Hill, 2018)
Source: Photo by a participant.

project. 'Maybe we can help them integrate into a healthier lifestyle,' she sighed, 'but not everyone's ready, so you keep your distance in a respectful way.'

Location can also shape the internal dynamics of a squat. Different neighbourhoods have different atmospheres and present different opportunities, whether that's the layout of the streets or estate, the design of the buildings in that area, or simply the number of available (vacant) units. The politics and social outlook of the neighbours is also important, as is the centrality and density of support networks. In comparison to Grow Heathrow – which Wanda described as 'so far out that, once you go in, you don't come out! (laughs)' – Denmark Hill struggled with the opposite problem of being relatively accessible, meaning that strangers regularly turned up at the space and asked to stay.

Figure 21 A spongey chair – Wanda had been checking on the plants, but one day found it had been taken by someone to put in their room (Denmark Hill, 2018)

Source: Photo by a participant.

From an ethical and political standpoint, the disposition of squatters (who themselves have no 'formal' authority over the space) tends to be to avoid excluding people. However, practically, this isn't always conducive to maintaining a safe and secure 'home'. Wanda had one unusual story which had directly confronted their right to use not only the building, but one of the bedrooms:

> There was a situation where a girl came late one night and said: 'I used to live here and I've been travelling. I've just come back. I don't know what the situation is, but I just need a night to sleep.' And then the next morning, I left, and when I got back, she was in my room … I said: 'Hi, *who are you?*' … It took half an hour to talk her out of the room because I felt defensive, naturally, from the way she was being: saying this was *her* room so she has every right to stay and sleep there.

However, after initially feeling threatened by the stranger, Wanda managed to avoid resorting to simply asserting her own legitimate use of the space, and instead decided to negotiate by helping her to find another space in the building:

She said she needed some place to recharge over the next few days and I thought that was fair. So, I said: 'I'll help you find a space.' I put a bed in the corridor and put some cloths up around it. She started to calm down and be less aggressive. I just had some empathy towards her situation. I don't think she had any money to stay anywhere else.

Others in the squat were less sympathetic. One person argued that the stranger had been aggressive towards him, while another claimed that she was lying about living here before and therefore she needed to go. Wanda stood up for her, but the whole episode had shaken her confidence of the space:

So, was that when you put the lock on your door?
Yeah, that was it really, before that we didn't feel like we needed to.

2

The Politics of Location, the Location of Politics

Who has the right to use space in the city? In *From Sylhet to Spitalfields*, Shabna Begum shows how squatting vacant houses and flats during the mid-1970s in the East End enabled a community to find somewhere to live, but also to assert their right to be in London. As part of colonial commerce between the UK, Europe, and the Indian subcontinent, there had long been a sense of affinity for the Bengali community with Spitalfields. And yet wider property relations, by structuring who is or is not considered to have a legitimate right to be in east London, meant experiences of systemic discrimination in housing and employment, as well as racist hostility and outright violence on the streets. Here, 'racial regimes of ownership'[1] played out through the actions of neighbours, politicians, the media, and the National Front, spilling from the street through windows and doors, attempting to deny the community 'the right or ability to make a home'.[2]

Some of the Bengali community turned to squatting simply because they needed somewhere to live. Others saw squatting as a route to fulfilling strict housing waiting list criteria and demonstrating they had a connection to the area. Yet, even when some families were granted housing by the state, they were often put far away from the rest of their community. This opened families up to the possibility of racist neighbours who didn't want them in 'their' part of the city, responding with threats, property damage, or physical violence. Because of this, many turned to squatting even 'after getting secure tenancies ... deciding that the tenancy was not worth their lives and that the insecurity of squatting was preferable to the regularised and brutal violence that they encountered in isolated flats and houses, away from the Bengali community'.[3] The squats being turned into homes, largely by women who made the buildings habitable and tended to be at home during the day to defend the space, were integral for creating a politics of care and resistance in the community (mirroring the central role women played in supporting freedom fighters during the Bangladeshi Liberation War).

Forming the Bengali Housing Action Group (or BHAG, which means both 'tiger' and 'share' in Bengali), the squatters eventually took over a vacant housing block, the Pelham Buildings, where they were able to live together and self-organise to protect themselves *and* assert their rightful presence[4] in East End London. Or as Begum puts it:

> For Bengali migrants in the racially hostile East London of the 1970s, squatting was a claim to social housing *and* to the right to be able to feel safe in the city ... Bengali squatters challenged the narrative about who belonged and who had earned their place in the East End and, through their refusal to be dispersed and dispossessed, refused to accept whiteness as a proxy for belonging.[5]

Some might describe this as asserting a 'right to the city'. Against those forces which would dislocate, un-home, and displace communities, claiming a *right* to the city – its spaces, its resources, its location – is an idea which has been mobilised across many different campaigns in different national and urban contexts. Since being coined by Lefebvre in the run-up to the infamous May 1968 uprisings across France, it has remained unclear what the right to the city should look like in practice, but there seems to be a sense that it 'implies nothing less than a new revolutionary conception of *citizenship*'.[6] This is not, and cannot be, a citizenship defined by the state and notions of national 'ownership' over a territory. Instead, as Alex Vasudevan has argued, 'for squatters, the right to the city has always been a right to remake the city and transform it through hope, resistance and solidarity',[7] even if, 'for an increasing number ... the very articulation of an alternative right to the city ha[s], in fact, become a battle to realise a more basic fundamental right to be *in* the city'.[8]

'Citizenship' is an idea bound up with the Western nation-state and has been used, historically and today, as a technology of differential inclusion, hierarchisation of people, control, and subjection, which pre-positions 'non-citizens' as devoid of voice or agency.[9] And yet, the *everyday* performances of citizenship, including conflicts on the ground as to who does or does not belong in a space, also suggest that 'citizenship is being constructed and experienced in a multiplicity of sites both below and above the nation-state'.[10] A 'Janus-faced' concept,[11] citizenship is both the continual reproduction of state definitions of membership *and* a place where new subject positions and affinities can emerge. Like the right to the city, citizenship is also 'inextricably spatial',[12] and can therefore be strategically mobilised to push 'for alternative forms of belonging' in the 'politics of urban presences'.[13] Citizenship should be understood as the battleground where people fight for 'the simple fact of living in the city ... being part of the city'.[14] The radical practice of occupying space and home-making goes beyond and against normative and disciplining codes of citizenship to affirm presence, providing 'the grounds for new forms of solidarity'.[15] This is, in other words, an *insurgent* citizenship, one which actively 'disrupts established formulas of rule, conceptions of right, and hierarchies of social place and privilege'.[16]

So, what might it mean to talk of a 'squatter citizenship' in the context of contemporary London? The idea of a squatter citizenship was first coined with the 'auto-constructed peripheries' of South American 'squatter settlements' in mind.[17] The concept sought to reframe marginalised communities and neighbourhoods as 'a city of pragmatists', constituting 'the greatest and most dynamic resources in building and managing the Third World City'.[18] Against stigmatising and disempowering frameworks which denied recognition and city membership (i.e. citizenship) to squatters, the argument here was that citizenship could be claimed *without* formal property rights and *without* the state. This was about recognising experiences on the peripheries, 'particularly the hardships of illegal residence, house building, and land conflict' as 'both the context and the substance of a new urban citizenship',[19] which produces 'a confrontation between two citizenships, one insurgent and the other entrenched'.[20] Citizenship can be about claim-making on the state, as in trying to get citizenship status in order to access legal rights or exercising citizenship by engaging with governmental systems. But it can also be about self-determination and how 'too little attention is given to the current and potential role of local organization and processes in reducing urban poverty'.[21]

In his study of homeless encampments in the US, Tony Sparks argues that, in these spaces, 'practices of citizenship were not understood as a formal relationship between sovereign individual and state, but between individuals and the collective within the informal terrain of the camp itself'.[22] Such 'informal' spaces are where diverse stories and experiences of marginality coexist and interweave. As well as practical – if often temporary – responses to living circumstances, these are locations for encounters with difference which intersect and influence one another. Without the automatic exclusionary authority of the ownership model, there is potential to generate a form of belonging and a sense of commonality. Squatter citizenship needs a location to flourish, but it is also formed in the fight to hold on to that location. 'The occupation is an instrument and a personal resource', argue de Carli and Frediani:

> shared life in the building is the basic infrastructure that allows for transforming one's life conditions ... it is through the encounter of these diverse selves and their respective drives for change that new political subjectivities are formed ... eventually facilitat[ing] the emergence of new collective meanings and moments of political becoming.[23]

Squatting is a form of citizenship which enacts the urban from the ground up by claiming space, location, and belonging *without* waiting for state recognition. Squats provide platforms for encounter, organisation, expression, and creativity, which take on a politics when spaces for these things are hard to come by. But they do not do so in a bubble. London is made up of both centripetal and centrifugal forces which have direct effects on those living in the city. On the one hand, centripetal forces 'pushing inwards' have concentrated areas of advantage and disadvantage by stigmatising whole areas of the city, criminalising poorer neighbourhoods while 'fortressing' richer ones, and holding back investment in social housing (even while using public money for compulsory purchase orders and planning permission to facilitate financial investment).[24] This is then matched by displacing centrifugal forces 'pushing outwards', such as the movement of wealthy upper and 'creative' middle classes into the centre, which is pushing out existing communities through gentrification, or profit-driven plans for increasing residential density on housing estates, and which entail 'regeneration' schemes via which existing communities are evicted.[25] In this whirlwind, squatting is one way to 'stay put' and push back against those forces squeezing and pushing marginalised communities out of cities like London. Squats have the potential to act as a temporary 'eye of the storm', a location of momentary stillness in the middle of a swirling economic and political system that spits out the poor while pushing the rich into the centre.

FOCUS E15

The Radical Housing Network, which sprang up across estates from 2013 onwards, is a clear example of how occupying buildings can allow for not only resistance to dislocating forces but also the development of solidarity networks and affiliation. In practice, regeneration has translated directly into the eviction of communities on social housing estates. Many have been forced to relocate outside of London, and with the loss of location comes a loss of connection, proximity, and solidarity. But occupations can help to recoup this. In 2013, a meeting hosted by a squat in south London brought together activists, housing campaigners, squatters and ex-squatters, and saw the birth of an umbrella group connecting multiple campaigns across the city (and internationally). While it certainly meant some had to rub shoulders with others that they did not necessarily share politics with, this created a critical mass with a renewed confidence to fight for housing justice and, in late 2014, this came to fruition when the network connected with the Focus E15 campaign in Stratford.

One Saturday morning, I joined Focus E15 outside Wilkos on Stratford High Street. Every week since their first occupations in 2015, this group of activists and residents have set out their stall and hung banners demanding that Newham Council 'Repopulate the Carpenters' and arguing for 'Social Housing Not Social Cleansing'. It was when the mayor of Newham – Robin Wales – had actively gone after Carpenters estate for regeneration, that they had turned to direct action. 'Focus E15' was originally a mother–baby unit and hostel next to the estate, owned by the housing association 'East Thames', which has 'fucking shiny shiny offices that literally overlook the Focus E15 hostel ... glossy glossy glossy'. When Newham Council decided to cut £41,000 from funding that was going to East Thames, the housing association decided that they couldn't run the unit any more. However, speaking to an activist involved with Focus E15, this move could be seen as part of a bigger picture:

[Newham Council] was big on fucking gentrifying the area and I believe that they were trying to just remove everyone from the hostel. And the idea was to bulldoze and create some luxury flats. The mother and baby unit is a hostel specifically used at targeting young teenage mums and their kids who are in need of somewhere to live ... So, the mums took their position to Robin Wales [mayor of Newham Council]. He said: 'You need to speak to East Thames.' They said: 'You need to speak to Robin Wales.' Ping-pong-ping-pong-ping-pong. There was no one responsible. So, they got their eviction notice and [the Focus E15 mums] were like: 'Fuck this, we need to fight.' ... So, they came together and started doing occupations, which then led ultimately to the occupation of Carpenters estate ...

On the Newham Council website, the Carpenters estate is described in a language that sets it up as ripe for development. The discourse highlights its proximity to the Westfield shopping centre and Stratford Station – both of which received huge upgrades and investment as part of the 2012 Olympic games – boasting 'excellent national and international transport links ... Stratford will have even better links to London once the Cross-rail services start running.' The website is also quick to remind the reader of who the owner is, pointing out that Newham Council 'is the majority freehold owner of the estate', which 'was previously managed by a Tenant Management Organisation (TMO), with management transferring back to Newham Council in 2015'. As the property title belonged to the council, they claimed the right to regenerate, over the right of those who lived there to use the space:

> So, they went to Robin Wales and he said: 'If you can't afford to live in there, you can't afford to live in Newham.' So, they kind of realised that Robin Wales was the enemy. The first occupation, they went to East Thames who had a show flat at the time ... the whole 'legacy of the Olympics' is really important to people, it's fucking disgusting ... so they occupied the East Thames show flat and they had a party for their kids.

At the Carpenters estate – as well as at many of the other estate campaigns – those involved tended to refer to 'occupations' rather than 'squatting'. This may have been a tactic to avoid being stigmatised as squatters and dismissed along those lines, or simply a reflection of their occupation being part of their campaign to continue residing in and using that *location* rather than that particular building. But, more importantly, this was effective tactically. While trespassing in a residential building with the intention to reside is a criminal offence, it was still legal to occupy any building as part of a protest and therefore 'for all of these occupations a simple notice was posted: "This is a protest occupation: section 144 LASPO does not apply."'[26] The actions escalated. As well as protest marches and hiring an iconic London Routemaster bus to take their campaign to City Hall in central London; they also managed to list the (now emptied) flats in a programme for an 'Open House' event where Parliament was opening its doors to the public. By the time Newham Council realised, it was too late. The message of Focus E15 was clear:

> All of these homes are empty on the Carpenters estate ... It could rehouse everyone on Focus E15 and loads more and the council were like: 'fuck off'. So, they occupied it and they managed to negotiate with Robin Wales

to open up 40 homes on the estate for other people. It stopped becoming about them, it started becoming about the wider issue of housing Newham ... Robin Wales tried to sell it off to ... I think it was either Goldsmiths or UCL. There was huge protests by the students and then they dropped it in the end and left it. So, Carpenters ... because of the campaign, Carpenters has become this really fucking thorny issue now. Because it's now so much more symbolic than it was.

One particular campaign – 'Jane Come Home' – was sparked when a woman on the estate was being evicted from the house she had lived in her entire life and came to the group looking for help. They made the decision to occupy the flat, placing the banner 'These People Need Homes / These Homes Need People' outside. But during the occupation:

Jane left because the council rang up and said: 'We've got a home for you, off you go.' Jane left the house. [But] the police then came, knocked down the door, arrested the occupiers and took them in ... [that's when experienced squatters] came in like really fucking useful [during] this occupation. They're like 'The dogs are going to be here in five minutes' and, sure enough, all the fucking police turned up ... it's just something that you have with experienced housing campaigners. It's incredible how quickly people can kind of ... know their rights and things.

Here, the connection between the community living on the estate with other campaigners, activists, and squatters across the city, was clearly invaluable, both in terms of finding support and solidarity to resist eviction, but also practically to know things like how to crack a building, how to barricade, and what your legal rights are.

Gillespie, Hardy and Watt argue that the Focus E15 occupations demonstrated, simultaneously, 'the gendered nature of the urban commons and the leadership of women in defending them from enclosure', as well as 'housing activism at the city scale' and an 'Olympic counter-legacy that is characterised by the forging of new relationships and affinities'.[27] While the occupation only lasted for two weeks, in the context of austerity urbanism[28] and social cleansing,[29] the temporary occupations provided a space for 'ensuring relationships and sustained movement-building across the city'.[30] At the time of writing, the Carpenters estate remains empty; yet Robin Wales's resignation as mayor (replaced by Rokhsana Fiaz) was a direct victory of the campaign, as well as the rehousing of 29 mothers from the Focus E15 centre within the borough. This campaign also marked the beginning of occupations on threatened estates across the city, with particularly high-profile actions at the Guinness estate and Sweets Way estate in Barnet, as well as the Aylesbury estate in Southwark.

In 1997, Tony Blair had famously raced to Aylesbury after being elected to deliver his victory speech,[31] heralding a 'new urban renewal' through the doublespeak of creating mixed communities while stigmatising existing communities on 'sink estates'. By 2015, plans for 'renewal' by decanting residents out of Aylesbury seemed well under way, and the occupations began. Like Focus E15, Rowan Milligan has argued that the squats at Aylesbury were important locations for relationships of solidarity and care to develop:

> Living side by side, day by day, creating bonds of affinity that could not be wrought through attending meetings and blockading gateways alone ... the bodily experience of eating together, with food brought up by residents by rope when we were blockaded in, of people turning up, asking what we needed ... beyond the concrete task of delaying demolition ... [they were] reigniting that sense of community destroyed by capitalist urban redevelopment.[32]

As someone who participated in the fight against regeneration on the Aylesbury estate, Milligan places a clear and strong emphasis on 'the physicality of an occupation, the feelings that are evoked from the concrete being in-common'.[33] Here, the legitimacy of being able to *use* the space wasn't founded in claims to greater ownership, but instead in the resisting of evictions and the protecting of one another from arrest. The community occupying the estate didn't assert their right to be there in terms of ownership (as in 'we deserve to stay because it's *ours*') but instead that 'everyone has the right to live here, even us ... [they were] expropriating a common space for whoever'.[34]

Squatting, then, is a powerful tool for creating common spaces, and there are many squatters who see this as the main purpose of occupying vacant buildings. Palmer, for example, is an active housing campaigner, environmental protester, and social activist, who was involved in almost all the housing occupations that took place around this time. Since first moving to the city after the financial crash in 2007/8, and after participating in Occupy (in) London, including squats at the Bank of Ideas and Occupy Justice, he had joined a crew who squatted a library which had been closed down by public spending cuts. On this occasion, their modest action had been incredibly successful. After occupying and renovating the library in Friern

Barnet, restocking the shelves, and reopening the library to the local community, they had managed to convince the council to allow it to be reopened on a volunteer basis, before handing the keys back to the local community:

> So that was another level of how to work with grassroots communities, how to organise people together to save something ... I started being something different, some kind of community organising grassroots activist ... I start[ed] more diverting power into funding and promoting solutions and connecting people into finding their own solutions to the crisis.

In 2015, he had joined the occupation against regeneration on the Sweets Way estate, dubbed 'Sweetstopia'. As he describes it to me, the estate had originally been occupied by its own residents after they had received eviction notices and before they connected with squatters like himself through Focus E15 and the Radical Housing Network:

> We went there to support them and connect and talk to the police and bring in the media. They were screaming for help. Our friends who organised them or helped them to organise, they were friends of us, one of them who we activated as a housing activist in Barnet. The other one was a friend of the E15 Mothers.

Squatting created synergies across the city; a clear sense of grassroots recognition and belonging. Knowledge and experience could be shared and brought to those facing the violence of being dislocated, while creating the physical and material spaces where solidarity could be nurtured. On the one hand, what the examples above demonstrate is that the occupation of space carries through the central ethics of squatting: to put disused spaces into use. But here, in particular, the use simultaneously asserts a politics of location against displacement by the market and state, and thus creates a location of politics, a physical and material space to nurture belonging, inclusion, and solidarity: a squatter citizenship. Through their occupations, the campaigners and squatters were able to assert claims to the space and create affinities which did not rely on the ownership model. There were no clear distinctions between 'resident' or 'squatter', 'political' or 'non-political'. And yet, stereotypes can still be casually mobilised and continue to shape (property) relations within these spaces.

DON'T BE A DICKHEAD

Figure 22 'Be yourself! But if you are a dick, being yourself will not help you' (TAA, 2018)

Source: Photo by the author.

From what I could gather, the housing occupation at Sweets Way estate had been far from straightforward. Palmer and I had first met at Occupy (in) London, and have kept running into each other over the years, but I got the sense he had become exhausted by recent campaigns: 'I burnt all my energy trying to make a difference in downtown.' He told me his laptop had recently been stolen while he was staying with squatters he didn't know, and the experience seemed to have left him quite bitter about squatting in London, which he criticised as being full of 'consumers', 'lazy idiots', 'party crews', and 'vampires'.

Palmer put it to me that a series of different occupations across the city had largely struggled to hold on to their location, because they had included people who do not take the politics seriously enough. While he seemed to embrace diversity as a political strength – 'we always had junkies ... but it was fine ... if people are *different*, they can make a *difference* (laughs)' – he bitterly complained of other types of squatters who took advantage and acted more like 'consumers':

> When we have to do an *open*-[door] campaign, then of course you can't stop people coming in, and it's good to have new people, but there must be some kind of safety net, because it's too much when you get sabotaged ... people are consuming maniacs. They feel they're entitled to things ... They will consume everything in their way over you. They're just *customers*.

Here, Palmer seems to be making a distinction between those he considered to be actively contributing to an occupation and those who seemed to take more than they give, perhaps by eating the food, taking up space, or even because of various support needs. Close to 'the consumers' were another type that he called the 'lazy idiots':

> Young people from pretty good backgrounds, middle-class youngsters who don't have enough money to rent, or they're smart enough not to rent ... completely idiots to this movement ... they absolutely knew nothing about what this is, nothing about squatting.

The problem here seemed to be that this group were not politically committed enough, and Palmer subsequently framed them as illegitimate users of squatted space. As well as taking housing and campaigns for public services seriously, Palmer had a particularly hardline on environmental politics and the climate emergency, and dismissed those he saw as 'party squatters':

> [They're] miming, or trying to mime, the basic comradeship of squatting ... they're not really *informed* and they're taking too much drugs as well ... they're pretty straight *compared to what we do* and especially on the environment side of the whole thing ... it's very decadent. They party like there's no tomorrow. We should *make* the fucking tomorrow.

However, he added that he did have some time for 'arty types', because 'art has a purpose... a changemaking force ... I mean if the artists are also lazy idiots, that's not the best thing, but if they are artists at least they are not consumers.'

By far the most problematic group for Palmer, however, was those who acted as 'despotic hierarchical oppressors' – or the *vampires*. He described this group as middle-class, educated, and usually having a reputation of being trusted or respected, but then they turned out to be 'part-time activists': 'They're buying a lot of vegan-branded shit and they save the planet ... [but] they don't stay, so they only show up every now and then to do one action, and they fuck off.' Apparently, the vampires *love* the idiots and consumers, because:

They knew nothing about anything. [The vampire] tells them to 'go there' [and] they just say, 'oh well!' (This is a person who's easily influenced, nowhere to go, perfect): 'this way please!' And then they start exploiting them and using them and pretend that it's a 'consensus based something' and 'good for the environment' or 'political' or something.

In his experiences at both Grow Heathrow and the Sweets Way estate, he described these occupations as becoming infested with vampires. At Sweetstopia, there was one individual in particular:

Our friend who was our comrade in the Occupy movement, turned from a liberal activist into a fucking despot. It was a bit strange the atmosphere ... He took out people's fuses if they didn't do what he told them to do, took their electricity and controlled them. So, they were asking 'When should we do a meeting?' And he's like 'no, no, no, no'. It's forbidden to say even 'community'.

In comparison, at Grow Heathrow, the evidence of 'vampires' was not reflected just by internal hierarchies, but in changing relationships with the local community:

I have emails from the locals saying that: 'Okay, if the bailiffs turn up we will come and fight ... but we're not welcome there [anymore], so we don't' ... The vampires did that for a reason. But now the vampires are gone, and the regime has collapsed (laughs). It's not safe for them because there could be bailiffs ... So, they left the people who we call idiots, who have still no fucking clue what they're doing there. So that's why there's even more gate-locking and less keys ... [We need] to get the locals back because the locals are the reason why it's there.

Here, Palmer argues that the very possibility of the squat acting as a basis for community solidarity is undermined by the 'vampires' who sought to exploit the space, control it, and subsequently undermine opportunities for inclusion and discussion by creating an atmosphere of isolation and distrust.

The consumers, the lazy idiots, the party types, and the vampires, all allowed Palmer to position himself (and others) as the *proper* activists, whom he described as 'soldiers' who were 'ready to die on the fucking spot' to maintain, fix, and defend occupied buildings, confront police, and fight landlords, as part of a broader mission to save nothing less than life on the planet. Referring back to the occupied library at Friern Barnet, he told me:

you're trying to help communities when you occupy something. You want to save ... once I stay in the library and if they came with a bulldozer, I don't give a shit. I'm going down with the building and I really mean it. I'm absolutely ready to die for what I believe in at any time. I don't give a shit. We need an army of people *who mean it*.

Each group that Palmer distinguishes reflect his perspective on correct or incorrect uses of the space, which can create exclusions (i.e. 'these people shouldn't be in this space') or hierarchy (i.e. 'their use is not as legitimate as my use'). Like all typologies, the risk here is over-simplification, giving the impression that these are groups of people that exist consistently across the city. It also creates a hierarchy of authenticity which, instead of acknowledging the different structural reasons for why people engage in squats in different and inconsistent ways, condemns people for a lack of commitment or sacrifice. Palmer's model raises crucial questions around accountability and how squatted spaces are being organised, including the politics of which uses and users are being recognised in which locations.

Another squatter, Mace, also referred to different types of squatters, but in a much looser sense. With residential buildings becoming trickier to squat, he pointed out that they were having to make use of much larger commercial and semi-commercial properties, sometimes on the fringes or far from residential neighbourhoods, which changed their relationships both with communities and each other. In this context, Mace referred to 'the dickheads' – a catch-all term used across multiple squats to vaguely describe annoying, disruptive, or violent individuals who take advantage of open spaces. As Mace explained:

> The fact that you can't just get in a house, like a three-bed house ... you might only have like three or four people occupying a place back in the day. Whereas *now*, you have to shoot for much bigger buildings by the nature of it being non-residential. So that kind of necessitates bigger crews working together... Because you've got to, you know? If you've got a big fuck-off warehouse and loads of offices, you don't want to just have three or four people living in it, it's not the best way to occupy the space, is it? You see the beauty of the group that we had [before] was because we all lived together ... because we all lived in the same *area*, we were tight ... you trust each other. Everybody knows they're on the same page. You can get rid of the dickheads that are causing problems in the group.

Bigger building means bigger crews which means (potentially) having to tolerate 'dickheads', especially in a context where squatting had become more precarious, more hardcore, and therefore has reduced the numbers of people willing to do it. In contrast, Mace distinguished those he imagined to be 'real squatters', who were willing to put themselves on the line to open and defend buildings. However, in contrast to Palmer's militancy, he framed this more as having direct benefits for forming trust and solidarity:

> Squatting really unites people. It binds people together in a lot of ways because there's the element of actually cracking a squat – which has like, an element of danger, you've got to put your neck on the line a little bit, you know? You could get nicked doing it. I know people that have got nicked for burglary because they've had tools on them going down a street ... it's *exciting* you know? It's good fun when you get into a place... And all this kind of makes for good cohesion with the people that are living somewhere ... it's like a product of your own action, isn't it? Which is like an *empowering* thing ... you've got to work together to do work on the building, you've got to work to people's strengths within the group that's living together. So, some people will be able to put a shower in, some people will be able to sort a kitchen out or ... you know? You have to work for each other and it's very much a collective endeavour, isn't it?

By allowing people to live together in the same building and the same area, Mace saw squatting as creating locations for collective endeavour and self-organisation, but in a flexible manner which allowed a crew to stretch and retract depending on the particular building, location, or energy of the squatters involved at any one time.

However, while Mace's account was not as strong or clear-cut or damning as Palmer's, hierarchies did creep in. For instance, he spoke about a hierarchy of skills, where those who had the experience of 'cracking' (i.e. opening up) or renovating occupied spaces gained some informal authority over the space:

> Sometimes people [with skills] will try and protect that knowledge and kind of keep it ... so there can be kind of like hierarchies within that. If somebody's good on the electrics then they'll try and ... I mean I've seen it happen, it's not all the time, but you know people will take that on and kind of ... jealously guard that job. I mean there's always kind of like those kind of skills hierarchies and it is kind of gendered as well sometimes. It's generally men that will be kind of keeping stuff for themselves and kind of enjoying the status that that brings. It's kind of esoteric knowledge isn't it? Doing electrics, it's kind of a bit dangerous. To some extent you *do* need somebody that knows what they're doing and you can't just have somebody that doesn't know what they're doing trying to do wiring ... it's like very *subtle* kind of status.

However, while recognising the hierarchies and power differentials this created, Mace also made a sharp contrast between those who brought much-needed specialist skills to the space, and 'freeloaders':

> You need to make yourself valuable to the group. That is important because, on the one hand, you can't have somebody that's just freeloading. That just fucking rocks up and says 'Oh ... I'm just going to fucking sit on this sofa for two weeks and then not leave and then do fuck all and be useless.' Because they're *useless* (laughs), right? But then, on the other hand, you don't really want ... you can't really have somebody either that's kind of you know, doing that *authority* and saying that they're more important than other people in the group because of whatever ...

Mace himself was heavily involved with the artistic squatting group Temporary Autonomous Art (TAA). In advance of TAA 2019, at an open organising meeting I attended at the London Action Resource Centre

(LARC), there was a disagreement around what the date for the next event should be. Attempting to facilitate a horizontal discussion, some of the more outspoken individuals insisted that we *shouldn't* take a vote, as this would create a majority and minority, and that we should instead reach a consensus on a date. However, inevitably, not everyone could make every date, and after hours of back and forth they simply chose the weekend that Mace was free, because he was the person who had the skills and willingness to go and crack the building.

The location of TAA was also a matter of contention. In the past, some TAA events had been more centrally located, which attracted a bigger audience and made the event more accessible, but also meant there were more people there who were not as 'invested' in the event. Ultimately, limited by where they could find suitable buildings, the 2018 and 2019 events ended up much further out of the centre, which meant that the people who attended were much more invested and 'hardcore':

> So last year [2017] it was in Hoxton and we were in the building and we had no problems in the building and there was a lot more kind of 'fluffy' artists turned up that maybe weren't so overtly anti-capitalist or whatever. They were just artists. Which is great as well. But I think this year because the building was maybe a little bit *hotter* – in a little bit of a rougher part of town – it was kind of different groups or crews of people turned up to go for it. And maybe a little bit more militant … it was a bit rougher. I don't know if people had heard about what was going on with the building. It was a lot more short notice as well. So, I think it needed people that were like dedicated and really wanted to go.

Here, the politics of location plays out *within* the squatting movement, playing a direct role in where they are able to find vacant and suitable buildings for different purposes, as well as who is able to participate and who is considered committed enough to travel out of the centre of the city to more far-flung and isolated parts of London. For Palmer and Mace, squatting allowed them to be part of a dense urban network by providing spaces and freeing them from the wage–rent vortex, but it also came with a set of challenges which they sought to pin onto different 'types' of squatter. Ultimately, however, it could be argued that their use of different buildings was shaped by location, including how central or peripheral they were, and who they end up sharing that space with.

PIE AND MASH

Figure 23 'Developers and Bailiffs Our of Our Areas' (Deptford, 2019)
Source: Photo by a participant.

Because their first squat was in a former pie and mash shop, the crew took the name 'Pie and Mash' with them, but it was also an ironic nod to the cockney rhyming slang – pie and mash, fash, fascist – which the anarchists who created the space thought was amusing. It was also a hint at their aspiration for the squats, given that the original pie and mash shop would have been a community meeting place but had been forced to close down by a steadily gentrifying high street. Oz had moved to Deptford from Forest Gate and invited me down. He kept referring to the Pie and Mash squats as 'the project', because every time they were evicted from one space, they simply packed everything up and moved it down the street to the next empty unit:

> The thing that was cool was, because we knew the area… we know where we are going, we know what we are doing… And every time we got evicted, we'd wait until someone got the [next] building open, then we'd just grab everything and march down Deptford High St in front of everyone … 'Oh, we're just going to the new place!' And then we'd take everything we could: the signs, the posters, everything that wasn't painted on the walls … and just be like 'Right, it's going to take us two seconds to set up.' The same stereo. Everything.

Figure 24   Reginald House (Deptford, 2019)
Source: Photo by a participant.

Oz argued that one of the reasons they were able to do this was because they had built meaningful connections with the area. Before the first squat, there had been a long-running campaign to save Tidemill Gardens (one of the few green spaces in the area), as well as nearby Reginald House (a social housing block), which were both slated for redevelopment. When it looked like the demolition might go ahead, local residents and squatters moved into the gardens to protect the space, and when the council got a court order to evict them, 'that's when people took to occupation: taking the trees, securing the front entrance, banners strewn across it all.' While ultimately unsuccessful in saving the gardens, this was the spark for a new community:

> When Tidemill Gardens got destroyed, we went back – everyone from Tidemill Gardens, all ages and colours, occupations – all went back to one of the local squats that used to exist on the high street. And people were furious: 'We're going to do something and take our own space! If they're going to take away the community space, we're going to create our own!' It was people coming together saying: 'We're going to take a space and it's going to be a neighbourhood space.'

When the first Pie and Mash squat opened, then, 'it came off the back of a decision by the local community to open a neighbourhood-wide space'. In total, four Pie and Mash cafés opened along Deptford High Street in the

Figure 25   Pie and Mash 4 (Deptford, 2019)
Source: Photo by a participant.

space of six months, creating social spaces and maintaining a presence in the neighbourhood:

> It was a well-established community in the sense that the people coming along to the café ... it was no longer just 'the people who had opened it up' making coffee for 'the people who had come to sit down'. The sound system was just brought by someone who just came in and someone else brought all their CDs. Then other people put them on and were the DJ for the afternoon while everyone was sitting down. People would run over and get each other tea and coffee. We never had to go and buy stuff, it was brought in by people who would come and hang out in the space.

The space opened twice a day for a few hours and provided free food, tea, coffee. They also put on quiz nights, board game nights, and gigs. While the crew were 'homeless people, squatting to house ourselves' in the space, they were also creating something public-facing where 'everyone came together'. That's not to say there wasn't some push-back:

We got attacked by some right-wing Millwall [football club] people because we had a bunch of anti-fascist flyers. They came back one night at one in the morning and started smashing it up, broke all the glass on the front door ... saying they were going to kill us sort of thing ... that's kind of the risk that you take when you expose yourself to the world. [But] I would like to do it more than we do ... it always feels good when you get a positive response and quite often you do get a positive response when you put these banners up ... There's not many squats out there with signs like: 'Fuck off, we live here, fuck off, we hate this neighbourhood!' (laughs)

Differences between the crew and 'public' became blurred in the space. One of the first people the squatters entrusted with a key was himself homeless and from the local area, and they encouraged him to run the café without them. This symbolised not only trust and an extension of responsibility, but also an ethics involved in opening up the space to the community. This created some issues in practice, but was also important in terms of maintaining the space as an open and inclusive community project:

You can't just expect people you know from the street to have the same [anarchist] principles. We tried to talk about horizontal organising principles, how we do things ... [but] sometimes there would be these interesting moments where someone who we have invited to come and take space there would be like: 'Oh, I'm running the space now ... OI YOU! SHUT UP OR I'LL KICK YOU OUT!' It's like ... 'No, that's not how we do things' (laughs). But hey, that was the beauty of doing this together. All these people who had different views, different lived experiences.

By breaking out of the wage–rent vortex, the crew had not only created time to take part in local housing and anti-gentrification campaigns, they had also been able to stay *located* on Deptford High Street. Despite the evictions, the series of spaces had facilitated the forming of bonds and relationships that were about to become invaluable.

'Going on from here', Oz paused our conversation: 'just to say, there was a lot of people involved in the project. So, when I talk about what happened, it's only from my own perspective.'

In early 2020, the UK government's response to the looming Covid-19 crisis was cavalier to say the least: with Prime Minister Boris Johnson openly shaking hands with infected patients in hospitals and appearing on national television to argue that the virus should be allowed to sweep through the

Figure 26 A zine reading group (Deptford, 2019)
Source: Photo by a participant.

population and create herd immunity. Meanwhile, Personal Protective Equipment (PPE) stocks had been allowed to dwindle under Conservative-led austerity, while the National Health Service (NHS) had suffered funding losses for over a decade. The infrastructure needed to deal with a pandemic was woeful even before it had begun.

In the early days, Pie and Mash 4 had to make a difficult decision. It was clear that the virus was going to cause widespread illness and death (even if the government hadn't really admitted this yet); however, at the same time, the café was not only their home, but the only free social space that many people from the neighbourhood had, where they could get something to eat, keep warm, or find company. Not wanting to risk people's health, the crew made the decision to close the café *before* the lockdowns had even been announced:

A lot of the people that were attending were people with disabilities, immune-compromised, not in good health in general. We thought it was a responsible decision that didn't rely on government instruction ... and explored other options of what we could do to utilise the energy in the neighbourhood.

Inspired by other activists in London, they decided to set up a mutual aid group from the space. Pie and Mash was particularly well positioned to do this in Deptford, Oz pointed out, 'because it was something in the neighbourhood a lot of people could relate to ... there was an affinity that had been built with people ... we already had the connections.' Through the squats, they had developed a location for politics, a distinct social geography, which could now be mobilised for mutual aid. Not only did they already have a support network, but they had somewhere to live for free, which allowed them to dedicate all their time to coordinating supplies and supporting vulnerable people in the area, acting as a hub for donations as well as storing, sorting, and cooking food.

In the early days of the Covid-19 pandemic, Pie and Mash spontaneously set up nothing short of a grassroots logistics network that didn't require the kind of corrupt contracts being handed out to Conservative party donors. They put out a call for donations and contacted supermarkets for surplus food, as well as 'skipping' food from bins (although they always checked whether people didn't mind received food from this source). Some volunteers started setting up spreadsheets to figure out all the different sources of food, when different shops were open, who contacted them last, and which days they could go and collect stuff. They even began sourcing donated fridges and freezers, intending to store perishable items at the Pie and Mash squat. Under calamitous and contradictory advice from the state, the Pie and Mash crew 'were doing what they [the government] couldn't, and they could see how much the community accepted it'. They were even listed on the council's website as a community group that people could turn to and were awarded a Lewisham Mayor's Award for community service (although, in true anarchist style, 'someone burnt the certificate').

With a monumental task ahead of them, they decided they needed to get more people involved and sent out an invite for volunteers to come for a meeting... 'and it was that morning we got evicted'. Despite the Covid warnings they had pasted on the door, the bailiffs smashed it open wearing masks and gloves. Oz speculated that the landlord panicked and wanted to get the squatters out *before* the eviction moratorium came into place (although when this did eventually come in, it explicitly excluded squatters, which 'left us as the only people who could be thrown out on the street in the middle of the Covid crisis ... as a friend of mine said, you could be thrown out on the street, and then threatened with breaking Covid [lockdown] rules').

Luckily, 'The Field' – a social centre at New Cross that had some more stability in using their space – offered use of their hub for the mutual aid network to continue, and within one week they had managed to get a regular public food stall in Deptford square:[35]

> So, obviously in defiance of the council, the police, and the government, we set up these stalls. Everyone wore masks. Everyone wore gloves. We got tape and chalk, set up 2-metre lines to make sure people weren't too close. Those of us who were the 'live-in' Pie and Mash crew, we opened another squat just to house ourselves in Lewisham. And we also used that as a bit of a place for the collections for mutual aid as well, because The Field at New Cross is quite far away and we had more space so could collect more stuff. And then we would use bike trailers and stuff to cycle it back up to Deptford from Lewisham and distribute it all.

After two and a half years of running the street stall, the peak of the pandemic had passed and people returned to school or work, so the crew decided to consolidate their efforts by relocating Pie and Mash to The Field. But while it was 'the same faces that were at Deptford square who came to the Pie and Mash nights', Oz had some regrets that they had moved away from their original location:

> There were other projects going on, but they weren't based on the same affinity. People in the neighbourhood coming together. People weren't just there to collect food, at Deptford square, it was to be together. To talk. To organise ... It's a shame to lose that presence in Deptford square ... but it was evolving to the circumstances.

From the early days of the Tidemill Gardens protest, squatting had not only provided spaces which supported solidarity, but had allowed Pie and Mash to become an integral part of the community. Here, we once again see the proactive role squatting can play at a time of crisis. Through direct action, they were able to provide the space and time to contribute without any cost (even if it was almost scuppered by a strategic eviction on the cusp of lockdown). By being located in the area, they were able to draw upon the pre-existing networks they had created and use them as a resource when the people of Deptford needed it the most. Thinking back on the Pie and Mash squats, Oz compared what they had achieved to the uses these spaces were being put to now:

Pie and Mash one is still empty, and the council have destroyed the roof on the back bit to try and stop it from being used. Classic Lewisham Council tactics ... Pie and Mash two was a betting shop and is now a casino. Pie and Mash 3 was a betting shop and is now a casino. Pie and Mash four is still empty.

A HOSTILE ENVIRONMENT

In order to participate in a city, you have to be located there, but there are multiple centrifugal forces which are dislocating people from London. While gentrification and regeneration schemes are examples of one centrifugal force, another is migration status. In the UK, border policy has been shaped by an ideology of 'domopolitcs',[36] in that the country is imagined as if it was owned, as if it was a 'home' belonging to some but not to others. In 2013, the racist 'go home van'[37] signalled the start of Theresa May's hostile environment policy, when she sent mobile billboards around ethnically diverse parts of the London, encouraging people without leave to remain to come forward for deportation. A series of governments have made it their explicit aim to make UK cities inhospitable to 'outsiders' on this basis.

Meanwhile, in Wandsworth, there is a dilapidated Thai restaurant which has been left empty since that van was driving around. The squatters had moved in just before Christmas. Having initially slept in the main restaurant on the ground floor, they had found their way up a fire escape and into the empty flats above. This carried a greater risk of quicker eviction (being residential space), but they were well disguised by the clearly abandoned ground floor. I messaged Xander to let him know I was here, but he was out. Instead, he let Anele know I was outside, who cautiously opened the door and introduced herself before we went down the side alley, across a tiny courtyard, and through the back door.

The décor was stuck in time, but the artists and students who were now living here had livened up the space with Christmas decorations liberated from bins, as well as original artwork. Where there had once been dining tables, we sat down on some old sofas, and Anele began sharing her story of coming to London to seek asylum. Returning to Zimbabwe after attending school in the United States, she faced hostility and potential violence (although she was not comfortable telling me, a stranger, why). Anele had therefore made the decision to flee to London because she had some contacts in the city who could set her up with short-term accommodation on arrival. However, this soon became untenable:

I had been living with friends and family and I could see that it was really starting to kind of ... add pressure to them. The Home Office wasn't getting back to me in terms of my asylum decision. I guess people were thinking: 'Ok, are we going to have to take care of you for the next five years? Six years?' So, I started talking to a friend who was a property guardian. And I say to them, 'I have no idea where I'm going to live and what I'm going to do, could I do something like what you do?' And he was like 'Well, why don't you just *squat*?' So, he introduced me to Xander. I met him and spent the day with him. I thought he was agreeable so like: 'Ok, yes, I'll come live with you and whoever else!' (laughs)

While waiting for the Home Office to decide her fate – that is, whether her application to remain in London was 'legitimate' or not – Anele has the status of an 'asylum seeker', which allows the UK government to avoid their legal obligations to recognise 'refugees' under international law. An 'asylum seeker' is held in perpetual limbo. Unless set up under a specific programme (as was the case with Ukrainian refugees), it is common for the first application for the right to remain to be rejected. In the meantime, applicants have no right to work and are not allowed to access formal education or employment. They are given a very small amount of money to survive on (Anele was on £35 a week) and if they do not have an address, applicants are usually given temporary accommodation in detention centres:

So [the Home Office] ask you: 'Do you have somebody to live with?' And I obviously said yes. If you don't have the option of that, then they put you in a detention centre 'while they're looking for suitable housing in which to place you'. I'm a single woman [but] I've got no children. I'm not a priority of their housing placements. And having heard the horror stories of the detention centres ... it's more like a *prison*. I didn't want that. So, I'd say 'I've got a place to stay'. Initially, I was staying with family and friends, but as it came closer to a year of staying with [them], the arguments started ... it was really bad.

As the Home Office dragged its heels, the hostile environment began to seep even into the temporary accommodation Anele had managed to sort out with family and friends, forcing her to consider other options:

I was talking to people. Some people were like: 'Well, there's a lot of people who get a tent and you can sleep in a tent.' But I didn't want to do that because I guess I felt it wasn't safe as a woman ... Also, if I'm caught then the Home Office would use that against me, so I didn't want to do that. There was also an option that someone mentioned once, which is you could just take the bus. Everyone talks about this one bus because it's probably the best ever ... it can literally take about two hours. So you can sleep for the two hours there and the two hours back: you've got four hours sleep! But I also didn't want to do that, so squatting seemed like the best.

When Anele told friends that she was planning to squat, they were really worried about it, with one warning her that squats are for 'drug dealers and people running away from the law'. But with a lack of options, squatting provided not only shelter but *some* freedoms while she tried to stay located in London to see through her application for refugee status. In a hostile environment, Anele found some sanctuary in squatting:

I have my own room! I have privacy. I have access to a kitchen. I have access to a bathroom. I have people I can actually talk to and do activities [with] ... it feels like family. You can see our Christmas tree? Over Christmas we cooked and we all stayed here and we ate. Just had our own Christmas party. And that's nothing I could ever have if I was in a tent or if I was in a detention centre.

Squatting gave Anele *some* relative comfort and freedom compared to her other accommodation options. 'Many people squatting' points out Cattaneo, 'wish to be masters of their time',[38] and Anele was able to live something of a 'normal' lifestyle, which contrasted strongly with her legal precarity, which was only allowing her to make London her home until further notice:

The best thing for me is the mental stability that [squatting] actually provides. When I want to be by myself, I'm in my room. When I want the company of other people, I've got that. I have the freedom to come and go as I please... to feel like I just need to take a walk and clear my head and I can do that without signing out or telling anyone where I'm going. I like the fact that we can go skipping! (laughs) I get sometimes to eat stuff that I probably would not be able to afford like ... cheese! This is a really nice neighbourhood, right? So, we got Waitrose [supermarket]. It gets rid of really cool stuff.

The location of the squat meant that the crew not only had access to up-market supermarkets but also parks to walk in and friendly neighbours – i.e. the types of things which make a neighbourhood a sought-after place to live. However, Anele also found herself having to navigate the stigma of squatting while living there:

Across the street is the pizza place. I was really really hungry and I see these guys all the time and I was trying to haggle with them, saying 'You're about to close, it's one in the morning!' And they're saying 'Come on, we close at three.' (laughs) One of my squat mates, he's very ... *arty*. Half-shaved head. He walks in and I'm like 'Hey!' And these pizza guys become really protective: 'Do you know that guy? Do you need us to walk you across the street?' And I'm like 'Actually, I live with him!' People get really shocked because I think they expect me to not look the way I look ... I say: 'I live in that squat' they're like 'Why?!' or 'Really?!' But people have these really weird perceptions. I have a friend who wanted to hang out, but I have no money, so she sent an Uber to come and get me. An Uber Exec, a Merc [Mercedes]. It parked by the loading bay there and I came out. The Uber driver when I get in says to me: 'So, you're going to work?' And I was like, 'No? Just going for dinner.' He thought I was a 'working girl' because I live in a squat.

Being located further out of the centre of London seemed to bring less unwanted attention to the squat from police, landlords, and critical neighbours, which potentially allowed them to stay there for longer than usual. The crew had even felt confident enough to open the space as an art exhibition to the public and had also supported a protest against the arrest of some Extinction Rebellion activists being held at the police station a few doors down, inviting them out of the cold for tea or to use the toilet. It was clearly important that they used the space as more than solely somewhere to live:

We had an open day where we just opened the door and anybody could come off the streets ... we had different people come in. We had one guy who volunteered to be a DJ so we had booming music ... people sat around and ate. It was amazing. I wish we would do more of that. I think this has been ideal space because, if you've noticed, the living space is very separated from the bit you can open [to the public]. So, you find that you can open up this part of the squat and whoever does not want to participate can still be in the living space ... other squats are not structured in the same way.

Anele's personal legal position meant she had continual background anxiety while squatting, concerned that living in a legal grey area might compromise her refugee application. As well as squatting what could be considered a 'residential' space in the flats upstairs, other associated criminal acts might have included inadvertent property damage when entering a building or being accused of stealing utilities. Anele wrote to both her solicitor and the Advisory Service for Squatters (ASS), who had assured her that squatting was not illegal, but that she had to 'stay on the legal side'. Despite initially being 'really afraid of the legal implications', Anele found that the crew she had joined responded with solidarity when she was open about her concerns.

When you're an immigrant, a lot of things can be used to deny you the rights you're seeking. So, I sat down with everybody when we first moved in and I was very open and honest about who I am and what my legal situation is. And everyone has been extremely supportive. I've told people that I can't open buildings. I can't break into buildings. I would also prefer not to do the initial holding of buildings and then move in at a later date. Everyone here understands and they've understood from the beginning. They've been extremely supportive.

When they had contact with the owners, Anele told me, she tended to make herself scarce, but 'everyone understood that'. She also tried to make herself useful by scouting for new buildings they could potentially occupy in future, wandering around the area, peering through the windows and checking for signs of vacancy.

The court hearing for a possession order was set for a few weeks' time. Despite some of the crew being very experienced squatters, they had somehow forgotten to register with the utility companies to pay for the energy supply, and many had had electric heaters on all winter to fight the cold and the wind which whipped through gaps in the rotten window frames. The landlord might not ever have realised people were living there had the electricity bill not landed heavily on their doorstep. With the eviction on the horizon, I asked Anele how she was feeling about moving to a new space:

I'm really anxious. I think I'm more anxious than everyone else. Everything that I'm going through right now, there's so much instability in my life, and this [squat] has been the *one* stable thing that's kept me really calm. Knowing that I have a roof over my head and people ... I just want to know where I'm moving to next. Even if it's like really crappy! I want to know where the next roof over my head will be. I'm definitely *not* going to show up at court [for the hearing]. I still want to think that [squatting] is easier than all the other options. Folk here have become almost like family. It's still so much better of an option than anything else ... I just feel like more people should squat. More people should open up their buildings. Just go for it.

Despite the precarity of squatting, it offered Anele a way to stay located in London and space to start building her life alongside her squatting family. In squats, she had found some agency and freedom, but also care, support, and solidarity, which was wholly absent in the wider hostility of the UK immigration and border system. Stability is relative. Without squatting, Anele would have ended up rough sleeping, or in a prison-style detention centre, while waiting for her right to stay in London to be formally recognised by a system reluctant to do so. Squatting gave her the opportunity to remain. She was able to stay put and assert her 'rightful presence',[39] not only to continue living in London, but to continue participating in the city as a squatter citizen while the Home Office kept her in limbo.

SQUATTER CITIZENSHIP

'People do not only live in homes' Madden and Marcuse point out, 'they live in neighbourhoods and communities ... they occupy buildings, but also locations in the social fabric.'[40] Recognising the politics of location is therefore crucial, both in terms of understanding those wider forces which are dislocating communities, and also the way in which squatting can provide a counter-location for politics: spaces for solidarity, belonging, and community. As the examples shared here have shown, *where* we live is as much about the particular characteristics of an area, its connections or isolations, its collective affinities or divisions, its centripetal and centrifugal forces. Urban policy frameworks 'have acted to "spin" poverty outwards to the urban margins',[41] un-homing people across the city.[42] But through squatting, communities are (literally) finding ways to stay together. Or as Heddy put it to me at Holloway Road:

[squatting] will keep the poorer people in London. If squatting wasn't legal, I wouldn't be able to live in London, like no way would I be able to even ... without sleeping rough, I wouldn't be able to be in the city really, it wouldn't be an option. So, it will keep the poorer people in London ... having buildings as well, like, you've not just got the building rent-free, you've also got space to *actually do something* and you've got ... it facilitates people being able to meet each other as well ... it gives us the chance to actually meet people and form the community that might not even be there.

Across London, as in many other cities, redevelopment is being asserted as the 'highest and best use' of urban space, and yet is pushing communities out of their homes and out of their neighbourhoods. 'From east to west and south to north' Anna Minton observes, '[homes] are tipped for demolition in a process that advocates describe as "estate regeneration" and critics condemn as social cleansing ... communities are broken up and tens of thousands of people displaced.'[43] Holding onto location is about physically staying put and asserting a right to the city, but it's also about protecting a sense of belonging to a place and staving off the alienation of a community from their own space. After all:

displacement is not just about direct replacement of poorer by wealthy groups; it also involves forms of social, economic and cultural transition which alienate established populations. This can entail forms of slow violence, which render particular neighbourhoods less hospitable and accommodating to established residents, as well as direct and forceful acts of expropriation which the vulnerable and precarious seem least able to cope with.[44]

In her work on the Heygate estate in Southwark, which was demolished between 2011 and 2014 as an early instance of regeneration, Ferreri argues that 'before and beyond the material loss of home, the dispossession of low-income housing involves a deeper unmaking of the relations that constitute residents' emplacement and political legitimacy'.[45] As low-income social housing has been increasingly subjected to real estate speculation, this has led to insecurity, eviction, and the 'decanting' of entire neighbourhoods who are rendered as an 'uncountable, faceless entity that can be poured, like a liquid, from one container to another ... the term evokes a temporal, suspended dimension: neither evicted nor displaced, people are temporarily "decanted" with the promise of being placed more permanently somewhere else'.[46]

Yet Ferreri finds that, rather than arguing for a presumed 'right to *property*' in their fight to stay located, these campaigns 'repeatedly invoke a right to "propriety": to be treated properly, to be acknowledged as proper political subjects'.[47] At the same time as communities are being dislocated, they find locations for politics and unfolding narratives of extended family and neighbourliness, reclaiming time and history, as well as collective responses: organising, networking, and mobilising through occupations and protests (or what Ananya Roy might refer to as a 'politics of emplacement').[48]

In his work on the Calais 'jungle', Van Isacker argues that the domicidal evictions and demolitions of informal campsites functioned as a 'technology of citizenship both by physically destroying "undesired" dwellings and by socio-symbolically prescribing normative forms of spatial inhabitance'.[49] By squatting in the town, however, migrants continued to be present and 'contentiously inhabit' this location, in spite of the destruction of the camps, which helped to amplify 'the visibility of ... grievances, asserts the occupants as political subjects, and creates space and time for solidarities to develop'.[50] This assertion of emplacement is a stubborn refusal to be dislocated by wider economic systems and policies, but also an assertion of their legitimacy to be in the city *at all*.

Squatting has become more difficult and 'hardcore' as the need to crack bigger (commercial) buildings, has meant organising, coordinating, and living with bigger crews. This creates difficulties in terms of dealing with property relations within the space, including (often gendered) domestic tasks of social reproduction, the need to call out unacknowledged hierarchies and create accountability, and even the need to potentially identify and exclude those who are disrupting the occupation. Without the ability simply to point to formal ownership as a source of authority, which shuts down multiple claims both to a specific space but also the right to be located in the city at all, these property relations can be difficult to manage. Yet this is also the performance of property being allowed to exist in practice, on the ground. One which seeks to sort out *use* rather than *ownership rights*.

The ownership model holds a powerful grip on ideas of who is entitled to be in which location, and it often justifies this distribution of space through the lens of citizenship. 'Within modern liberal states,' argues Ananya Roy, 'access to property contains the promise of autonomy and full citizenship'.[51] Until the 19th century (men) and 20th century (women), property ownership was the only way to qualify to vote in many democratic countries. A lack of property title was also used to distinguish white 'civilisation' from indigenous 'savagery' and black slavery, with the assumption that whiteness legitimated the right to property title.[52] Many colonial laws, norms, and codes which continue to govern housing, building, and planning – and were originally designed to ensure political and economic control on behalf of the foreign power – remain unchanged in many postcolonial cities, while the development of new property technologies, which formalised ownership, such as land registration and surveys, 'promoted individual rights over communal rights'.[53]

Simply by creating a space over which no one can claim formal (exclusionary) ownership, communities under threat of being displaced can create new bonds, affinities, relationships of care, trust, and solidarities. In this way, squatting can free up space and time in which people can act as *citizens*, even in cases where they are being denied such recognition and legitimacy by the state. In contrast to the state and the market, squatters directly *contribute* to the city. They re-open community services such as libraries shut down by government austerity measures. They open cafés and event spaces which don't have expectations that people must behave as 'customers' to have legitimate use of the space. They act as hubs for mutual aid networks in the context of state incompetence, using time freed from the wage–rent vortex to support and care for the community around them.

Checking out an East Ham library

Figure 27   The Passmore Edwards Library (East Ham, 2019)
Source: Photo by the author.

From central London, you can either take the District Line or Hammersmith & City to East Ham station. Turn right down the high street. Past the shops and the restaurants. And make a left at the Sri Mahalakshmi Hindu temple. Go past the school. When you get to Plashet Park, keep straight until you get to the far corner where some men are sat afternoon drinking on the benches. It's here you will find the magnificent Passmore Edwards library.

I'd heard rumours about a squatted library out this way, but it was only when I met Xander at Temporary Autonomous Art (TAA) that he invited me to come over. This grade-II listed building was far from what I had imagined. John Passmore Edwards had been a typical Victorian philanthropist. Concerned with the liberal education of the population, he funded a series of ornate libraries across London with the aim of providing free education. Many of his libraries had remained open for over a century until they were closed by the Conservative-led coalition and their policy of austerity after

Figure 28 Living room (East Ham, 2019)
Source: Photo by a participant.

2010. Some were sold off and privatised. Others, such as this one, continued to be used as council offices before being abandoned, and now had the tell-tale signs of vacancy. The black-barred gates at the front were chained and padlocked, trapping windswept leaves and wrappers. The flower beds were overgrown. The windows were dirty and, except for the section 4 notice and a hand-written sign appealing for public involvement, there were no signs anyone was living there.

I heard a fire exit open around the side and out stepped Xander with his charismatic grin from ear to ear: 'Come in!' We stepped inside and he re-barricaded the door behind us, wedging a chair behind the handle. Down the corridor there was a small kitchen, then we entered the former staff room, which was right in the centre of the building. The tables had been pushed into the middle and were surrounded by chairs and sofas. At the back, an old bedsheet was serving as a projector screen, and someone was sat watching a boxset of *The Good Life* (which had been skipped from a bin behind a charity shop):

> Squatting is about recycling … there is just so much accumulation of things that are manufactured, and shipped, then just thrown away. It's unbelievable how common it is with food, with electronics, with everything … and it takes such a big toll on the environment. People don't value stuff. People

Figure 29 Working with what was already there (East Ham, 2019)
Source: Photo by a participant.

go to food banks, yet there's so much food being thrown away. It's absurd and it shows how society is broken.

The squatters were a mixed group of young adults, some of whom were 'in difficult situations, on the verge of being homeless, or struggling with some issues' but had found a safety net at the squat. 'It's our living room and it's just so cosy', Xander said:

> I see it as my home, but it's *temporary*. For me, [the library] represents something that's important for the collective identity of [East Ham] and I think it should be used for some sort of public function. I think there's a general agreement that the building should be used for something *constructive*. And once there is a plan for its use, it's alright for us to move out.

The squatters had regular house meetings where they attempted to make decisions by consensus. I was told that they had recently agreed to change the 'trial period' for new people joining the space. Whereas this used to be 14 days to see 'how we clicked' and to see 'whether this person is OK and not someone bad for group dynamics', they were now going to extend this period, because 'they can just be nice for 14 days, then things get tricky'. The aim was to keep a balance in the space between being 'open

Figure 30   The Making Space zine (East Ham, 2019)
Source: Photo by the author.

enough, but still able to protect yourself' and Xander had a fair bit of experience squatting in London where having an open-door policy simply had not worked:

> To me, it's important. It's a safe space that enables you to deal with some of your issues, or challenge some of your prejudices, without repercussions. To feel safe and at home, and not threatened by anything, is really important. It's interesting how rare it is to find a space like that. A space where you're not being asked to pay anything, or behave in a certain way, you know? It can be quite empowering.

We continued past the reception desk and a records storage room with a heavy fortified door. At the front of the building were two library reading rooms which had been turned into a mix of exhibition space, art studio, and a tattoo parlour. I was surprised to see my own zine on display boards, cut up and annotated. Xander explained that when they first occupied the building, they had originally wanted to open these rooms to the public as a social centre:

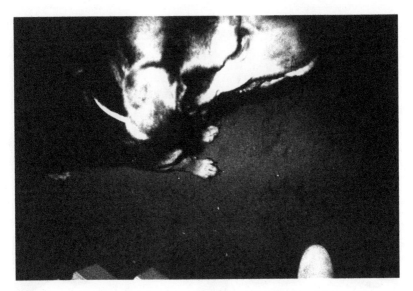

Figure 31   Sabba the squat-dog. 'She barks at everyone she doesn't know, I love her. She's the soul of the squat. The problem is, she barks at everyone but bailiffs (laughs).' (East Ham, 2019)

Source: Photo by a participant.

> We're quite an organised crew. And when we wanted to turn the library into a community space, there were some people making the effort, some people *not* making the effort, some people saying they were going to make some effort but not making effort in the end ... yeah, just different priorities and sometimes lack of communication ... Our first priority is to have somewhere to live.

As an artist and an activist, Xander was particularly motivated to pursue multiple uses of a space as somewhere to simultaneously live, organise, create, and open to the public. In many ways, he encapsulated the diversity of London's squatting scene within just one biography. Without squatting, he would either be sleeping rough or trapped in the wage–rent vortex:

> I didn't want to work full time. I really wanted to do my own thing. I wanted to be able to read and draw and paint. Just have a bit more freedom than having a full-time job ... Squatting is the reason I could commit myself to art and continue to get better. It's not my main source of income, about half/half. I also do part-time work [now] and work for agencies.

Figure 32   The table (East Ham, 2019)
Source: Photo by the author.

As well as free housing and studio space, squatting meant Xander could dedicate more time to perfecting his artistic skills, even though art did not (yet) provide him with a full income. 'For a long time, I didn't make any money for my art,' he explained:

> and squatting is helping with that massively still ... I was able to learn skills, to do projects, to meet people ... if I wanted to stay in London, the only alternative would be to work full time and that would not give me enough time to do all those things I wanted to do. It's squatting that allowed that.

Upstairs, former offices and storage spaces were now bedrooms. We climbed over someone's mattress and out through a window onto the roof. It was a glorious day and there was a clear view right across the park of children playing football in the sun. We looked down through the skylights into the living room and waved at some of the others sat around the table, chatting or skinning-up. Through fits of laughter, Xander tells me about when Rokhsana Fiaz – the (new) mayor of Newham, who took over from the notorious Robin Wales – had come to try and negotiate with them to leave

Dear neighbours

As you may already be aware, we are in occupation of this historical library. We are a diverse group of artists, students and workers from many areas of the globe. We are squatting this building in an attempt to promote the idea of squatting. We believe that squatting is a way of utilising empty buildings for living and community use which otherwise would be disused and would fall into disrepair. Many of the empty buildings in London have not been in use for many years and are largely owned by private corporations who use the building for profit, or council buildings which have been closed due to central government budget cuts, such as this building. We would like to prevent these places being closed down and turned into generic offices, luxury flats or parking lots as has been the case in so many buildings in London, instead to have these old loved community buildings reused for the people as originally intended. We would instead like to show that these buildings can still have a purpose for connecting the community, ran by people of the community, not by private companies for the purpose of profit.

By squatting this building we would like to show that squatting is a valuable legal tool to reclaim empty spaces for the community. We wish to foster a connection with people in the area as someone to support and be active in the community. As a group and individually we have been using empty spaces for many years. We have previously held art galleries, exhibitions, cinema nights, music jams and events, discussion groups, practical workshops, ran a project supporting the local homeless and providing free meals for people and many other activities utilising the empty spaces and the skills of the occupants and members of the community.

The Passmore Edwards library is a building named after the journalist, John Passmore Edwards who was an ardent supporter of the working class and erected many buildings in London for the purpose of the community. We think it is a shame that such a building has been left disused for years and would like to honour the memory of him by putting the space to use. We wish to preserve the building how it is as it is a beautiful piece of art and do not want it to be unsecured, destroyed by lack of care, time or being deformed by a company who does not care about the building and its history.

Whether we are here for a short time or longer, we hope to leave a positive impression in your minds and to help now and in the future.

Yours Faithfully;

Your neighbourhood squatters.

Figure 33 A letter to the public, posted on the outside of the library and signed 'yours faithfully, your neighbourhood squatters' (East Ham, 2019)

Source: Photo by the author.

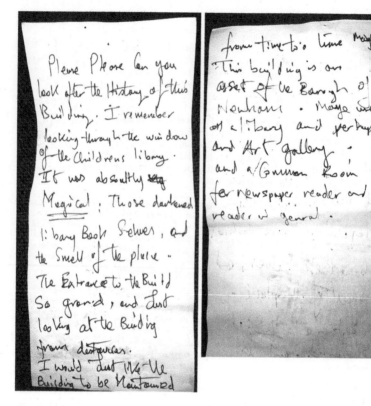

Figure 34 A note from an anonymous neighbour to the squatters: 'Please please can you look after the history of this building. I remember looking through the window of the Children's library. It was absolutely magical: Those darkened library book shelves, and the smell of the place. The entrance to the build[ing] so grand, and just looking at the building from distances. I would just like the building to be maintained from time to time maybe. This building is an asset of the Borough of Newham. Maybe used as a library and perhaps and Art gallery and a Common Room for newspaper readers and readers in general.' (East Ham, 2019)

Source: Photo by the author.

and someone had left king skins and a bong out on the table. Newham Council had offered the squatters a property guardian contract in a different building with a notoriously controversial guardian company, founded by someone who used to volunteer for Advisory Service for Squatters, that obliged guardians to do 7 hours free community work a week as part of their contract:

We refused Dot Dot Dot because they're finding a gap in the housing market. Essentially, what they do is charge the owner *and* the people who are renting the place. They are a mediator getting money from both sides.

Xander was very wary of negotiating in general. He pointed to Paris as an example, where authorities allowed artists to take over empty spaces on a temporary basis, but he argued that this then acted as a 'tool for gentrification ... they've lost their critical edge [and] it boosts tourism'. While he wasn't so hardline as to deny *any* negotiation with property owners or local authorities, Xander also worried that it compromised their political aspirations:

If you're negotiating, you're setting up the idea that the property is owned by one person, and they're entitled to that. Squatting challenges that, right? ... the idea of squatting is to challenge the idea of property ownership, London is a really great example of current property ownership policies not working at all.

Later, after they had been evicted, Xander reflected back on some of the challenges in the space, but still saw squatting as the 'logical option'. He had gained confidence dealing with the authorities and owners, and no longer thought it was a 'big deal' if the police came – 'If you get arrested, it's not the end of the world.' The everyday challenges of negotiating their use of empty property hadn't deterred him from wanting to open up more disused spaces, whether for living and/or for local communities:

It can be difficult. But it can also be a learning experience and fun. If people use buildings for other purposes, whatever it is, parties, exhibitions, community-run projects that are run 'by the people', rather than a centralised power like the council, government, or charity ... that's really good as well.

Xander's aim was to diversify unused spaces. On the one hand, the library was their home, but they were also acutely aware that it *should* be a public resource. The symbolism of the building, its history, and position in East Ham, as well as the political decision to shut down the space through public spending cuts, all weighed heavily on the decisions of the crew. However, they were more than willing to grapple with these problems and contradictions that come with navigating use on the ground.

3

An Aspiration for Space,
a Space for Aspiration

What kind of society do we aspire to be? Before even answering that question, there first needs to be a preceding one: who are 'we' and who gets to decide, shape, limit, or expand our aspirations? To reflect meaningfully on the future, we need the privilege of time. We also need spaces where different aspirations can be articulated, and where we might learn about different experiences and troubles across geographical and historical scales. Squats, as nodes which sustain networks, have the potential to work across different political scales simultaneously: from the neighbourhood and community. through to regional, national, international, global-existential, and historical. They are *centres* where people can converge, come together, organise, find a community, and be *part of something*. But at the same time, squats can *decentre*, by going with and beyond their particular location. Firmly grounded in the city, these 'zones of anticipation'[1] have the potential to inspire both a *sociological* imagination by connecting private troubles and public issues[2] and a *political* aesthetic by manifesting collective voice and appearance.[3]

Squatting is therefore valuable infrastructure for grassroots campaigns and social movements, a network of material spaces from which communities can form and organise. Across different cities and contexts, squatting has supported aspirations for change. Without these spaces, marginalised voices can struggle to get campaigns off the ground. While precarious, each squat acts as a temporary node which, even if it doesn't last long, has an influence which can reverberate, as 'each occupied building is a link in a chain of antagonistic struggle against dominant power structures'.[4] They are spaces where movements are made *material*, providing resources for collective organising and connecting, by *repurposing* a building and literally *reshaping* part of the city.

Social centres are a clear example of this. Originally emerging from Italy in the 1970s, Mudu argues that they were simply a direct response to a 'dramatic decrease in political spaces'.[5] With economic shifts away from secure careers and towards flexible contracts, he points to a loss of traditional locations where people would come together and get organised, such as the factory gates, university, or union headquarters. It was in these circumstances that people turned to squatting in order to set up self-managed spaces from which campaigns could be built and operated, while simultaneously focusing 'attention on land use issues and the struggle for re-appropriating social time'.[6] In this way, we might say that social centres support the development of squatter citizenship, insofar as they are:

> sites/locations where the occupants/activists organise radical/antagonist political and social protest campaigns ... addressed outside the squatted spaces, in the city, in the urban fabric and in the society at large ... they are urban actors because they are spatially localised ...[7]

What is characteristic about social centres is that they are, at the same time, a *location* (i.e. firmly situated in their locality) and a *network*, which enables actors not only to spread their campaign to various publics outside the movement but to converge, organise, and mobilise across multiple local, regional, national, global, and historical political scales. These can be sites for fighting inequality and discrimination (such as on gender, sexuality, race, class, disability, age), as well as sites for grappling with international and global-existential issues, such as anti-war campaigns, anti-capitalism, and action on the climate emergency. They are also spaces which can simultaneously tap into multiple issues by centring, contextualising, and connecting. The loss of a local park to development, for example, can be framed as both a *local* loss of public space for the neighbourhood *and* a loss of green space in the fight against global capitalism and the climate crisis.

Infrastructure can also be provided by non-squatted or formerly squatted spaces. These nodes have the added benefit of longevity and (some) security, in that they have a reduced risk of short-notice eviction. They can therefore not only provide some stability in grassroots networks, but their persistence in the space means they can build relationships with publics over time. These non-squatted or formerly squatted spaces are often referred to as 'infoshops' (although infoshops do also exist in squats). They provide space for meetings, events, offices, but also community services (such as bike workshops or selling affordable organic food). They are also hubs for sharing information, including books, pamphlets, leaflets, zines, posters, often accumulating these materials into archival collections. With their relative solidity, infoshops often act as spaces for the safe storage of archives, through which campaigners can be inspired from past movements.

Squatted spaces tend to have more flexibility than non-squatted or formerly squatted spaces, because they can more easily be adapted by the community occupying it. Whereas the landlord or property owner might object to plans by a group to remodel the layout of the rooms, or might not be interested in repairing the building, squatters in contrast are 'space producers, they manipulate places, providing new ones'.[8] Christine Wall's research on the Women's Liberation Movement in 1970s Hackney is a good example of this. She argues that squats were pivotal for feminist politics at the time, because not only did they provide free spaces where women could live – meaning they 'provided a ready solution to the poor provision of housing for single mothers and single women'[9] – but also a geographical density which 'enabled groups of feminist women to meet, organise, and discuss politics as part of daily life'.[10] Squats not only acted as housing and refuge, but work-spaces, nurseries, and organising spaces, which distinguished themselves from the patriarchal conditions of suburban life. The everyday experience in these women-only squats was facilitated by 'engaging directly with the built environment, adjusting, repairing, and adapting [spaces] by women and for women'.[11] Their aspirations for societal change and their material changes in the squats, in other words, were one and the same.

To take another example, there were an estimated 50–60 men living in gay squats along Railton Road and Mayall Road, Brixton from 1974 onwards. These communities were often connected with, and supported by, the Gay Liberation Front (GLF), which had wider political aspirations of 'a sexual and social revolution that would reconfigure familial, sexual, and emotional relations and abolish all forms of social oppression'.[12] As part of this goal, they reconfigured empty buildings in a way which materialised their politics. Inspired by GLF communes in Bounds Green, Notting Hill, and Bethnal Green, Cook describes how the community 'tried to jettison notions of privacy, private property, and monogamy' in order 'to provide a counter to the nuclear home and family which they saw embedded sexism, homophobia, and capitalism, inhibiting self-expression and exploration'.[13] Knocking walls through and removing fences between gardens, the squatters created communal living spaces which existed in direct contrast to the wider society they were campaigning to change. However, tensions sometimes arose within the space around whether the revolution was personal (i.e. something to be achieved within their squats) or something that needed to be more public-facing and out on the streets. While the communes undoubtedly 'helped to cement a sense of community', Cook argues that they also 'fostered a certain insularity'.[14] In other words, the very means by which they were able to establish spaces to live and push back against the heteronormativity of the city, also risked ghettoising their campaign and reducing opportunities to engage with wider publics.

In a study of the Rebel Dykes in the 1980s, Miller also found that ideological tensions flared between the 'radical feminists' (such as at Greenham Common) and anarchist feminists when the latter began to embrace punk, sadomasochism, transsexuality, and engaging with sex work. Moving into squats in Brixton, the Rebel Dykes were able to situate themselves spatially and politically, and challenge common understandings of lesbian and feminist politics through 'a coalitional array of sexual- and gender-dissident women'.[15] Through 'trespassing, mending, repairing, adjusting and adapting'[16] space, the Rebel Dykes, demonstrated how squats simultaneously '*make* place and space and are themselves *made* in and through place and space'.[17] 'Squatted spaces', argues Miller, 'are created in relation to – and are constitutive of – subjectivities, politics and relationalities'.[18] As such, squats can be, simultaneously, the means of aspiration *and* the ends which are being aspired to.

Squats have played pivotal roles in wider political campaigns and community aspirations. Below, we first focus on 'social centres' as an example of squatting that creates essential nodes in wider networks. Spaces are being created for a whole host of different campaigns and movements, which tend to be free to use and not carry limitations that might come from a formal contract or lease. However, because they are squats, they are also susceptible to quick eviction (although there are examples which have lasted an impressively long time). They can also struggle with public relations, insofar as they might be attempting to spread their campaign(s), but the very thing that has given them the space from which to do so – squatting – also carries stereotypes and stigmas that may make this difficult. We then look at 'info-centres', which *can* be set up in squatted spaces – but here I focus on examples of non-squatted and formerly squatted spaces where squatters have sought to negotiate with owners in order to sustain their use *and* the network(s) of which they are part. In the second half of the chapter, I will then demonstrate how 'squatting as a means' (i.e. to sustain wider campaigns) and 'squatting as an end' (i.e. where the occupation of the building is the campaign itself) are always intertwined. Even if the change they aspire to goes beyond the particular location of the squat, the very *context* of the city in which this space has been put back into use, entangles the wider campaign with the material of the squat itself. The means and the ends are always the same in squatting, even if this isn't always made explicit.

BLACK UNDERPANTS AND YOGHURT WEAVERS

'What I sometimes say is, I'm a socialist with anarchists, and an anarchist with socialists,' Bryan explained:

> But these days it's less necessary to say that, because actually the overlap is a lot clearer than it used to be … Socialists were kind of hide-bound by their procedures and their hierarchies and stuff, you know. 'Must have a membership secretary!' or whatever. And the anarchists were very 'oh, ya boo socialists… Soviet Union! Stalin!', you know. But that's much less the case since, starting in the 1990s, there were key hookups.

As well as living in and out of squats throughout the 1990s, Bryan's main involvement in squatting had been repurposing empty buildings to set up social centres. These were intended to be simultaneously 'public-facing' *and* to provide spaces for activists of diverse stripes to come together. Crews which establish and attempt to run social centres often aspire to engage with their local community, to put on social events and workshops, to share information, and to provide spaces for much needed amenities (e.g. libraries, nurseries, youth centres, internet cafes, bike repair). Because squats carry no hiring costs, and because no one who is using the space can claim formal ownership over the building (and what it can or cannot be used for), social centres often aim to provide spaces for local groups as part of their wider political goals for horizontally organised communities and grassroots organisation:

> Squatting is about just defending your space and trying to make it as liveable as possible. And a lot of that is *infrastructural*: being able to turn on the electric and wire that up … One of the *great* functions – apart from helping the homeless – of the squatting scene in London has been social centres … the fact that you can get a *free* community centre! All of the people I've met needed that place because they're activists. [Squatting] meant they could be 24/7 activists as opposed to doing a job at a pizza restaurant to pay the rent. So, it made them *useful* people. [Social centres] meant they could save money and put that to some useful cause.

Bryan recalled a few 'favourite' social centres he had been involved in over the years, which he had considered successful because they had made the most out of empty buildings which were otherwise being wasted, and engaged 'the public' with social and political issues:

[The Rainbow Centres] were in a church. It's beautiful, yeah. I remember we set up these 'Min-Cin' – a mini cinema – in like an old, recycled television, with a cheap old computer, and just ran all day.

One of my favourites was the RampARTs down in Whitechapel. That had all kinds of fascinating events. It was like an old school and, for some reason, the landlord was not very vigilant or just not there. And it lasted for what ... five years or something I think. That was really useful when we had the European Social Forum in London. Lots of people stayed there.

I mean, the Bank of Ideas had a very wide range of people coming through it. It was quite a *smart* property anyway (because it had been a bank). We had a TV studio there. It was nice. We could set up and lock it – you can't do that in a squat normally. We could lock the room and feel reasonable safe. And there was 'security' on the door ... 'helpers' on the door ... but there were ways of dealing with ... err ... disruptive elements.

Asher had also been heavily involved in organising social centres with Bryan since the start of the 1990s and had particularly fond memories of the Rainbow Centres as an early response to climate crisis:

We read some stuff about what was going on with the Rio Earth Summit [June 1992]. And I'd been reading bits and pieces about environmental stuff, and Earth First, and this, that, and the other. I went to visit a couple of other places, like the M11 ... Claremont Road. They had a little infoshop (basically a kettle and a few leaflets). Some other mates squatting up near Hampstead had this art gallery squat where the whole downstairs was covered in artwork. Another group out at Ladbroke Grove called 'Art Space/Live Space' ... became Invisible Circus ... they've now got seven buildings in Bristol that they're recycling, done up, got community art stuff going on, because they've got someone cooperative in the council working with them (shows what you can do, they got a charity set up). But I saw that they were putting on art space, creative art galleries, and living space ... and I came up with this idea for Rainbow Centres.

The Rainbow Centres were so successful that they even sought to formalise one of the spaces and get a lease so that they could carry on:

> Back in '92, we did business plans and tried to ask for a Rainbow Centre, a community centre. Islington Council was going to give one ... We were squatting some buildings up on the North Circular road ... so we had a bit of time, and waited for six months ... they were supposed to give us a reply, [the building was] supposed to go free to a community group that came up with a good proposal ... we were waiting for about eight/nine months, ages and ages, and then they gave us a reply 'No, we're not going to give it for free to a community group, we're going to sell it for a million quid!' So, we were really pissed off and like 'fuck this'. Went and squatted the big old church up in Kentish Town and probably one of the most famous Rainbow Centres. Got a deal off the Church of England. Had it for about two and a half years, packed it with events, parties, conferences, meetings, workshops, organised a lot of the road protest movement, and Criminal Justice Act, and all sorts you know?

The Rainbow Centres certainly hold a space in the hearts of many squatters from the same generation as Bryan and Asher. But, aside from the challenges of trying to hold on to a building from which to operate, the main difficulty for Bryan was actually that squatted social centres had to contend with the prejudices of the 'public'. By occupying spaces already familiar to the 'public' – a church, a school, or a bank – the façade and décor often carried more of a welcoming and respectable sheen. But by virtue of being a squat, they also struggled to challenge stereotypes of being dirty, unclean, unhygienic, and close to criminality. For Bryan, presenting a 'public' image of accessibility, making it easy and welcoming for people to get involved, was a crucial part of successful social centres:

> Free public space is really important. And I hope that we'll make [spaces] as unthreatening to people as possible, in terms of look and feel, you know? [For example] vegan food is great. Vegan food is cheap and you can skip it. Skipped food is great. Freegan/vegan food. The Bank of Ideas had free meals every day and any decent squat, community-open squat, has free or donated food ... We deliberately make [squats] as smart as possible. Somebody had skipped some fancy glassware and stuff like this. We'd have a bottle of cheap Prosecco or whatever. We'd have a fancy table-

cloth, this kind of thing. Like 'this is not a soup kitchen' you know? Partly a joke and partly taking on the whole squatter image.

The concern is that, by squatting, the campaigners might end up in an activist ghetto insofar as they find internal solidarity and recognition through a shared subculture, but which might be off-putting to others. Given that many squatters are partly motivated by a rejection of wider economic, political, and cultural norms, this isn't that surprising. Yet Bryan saw it as part of the mission of social centres to try and break out of this:

Squatting, squats, or *anarchist* squats, can be quite challenging for 'ordinary people'. There's always been an issue with me when setting up social centres or whatever. I come in as a 'culturally-conservative' type who doesn't want scary graffiti and the black clothing and the sort of grime-culture sort of thing. It's off-putting to the kind of groups who would come along, maybe groups on the local council estates, but instead there would be hippies. There would be more 'alternative' stuff. What we used to call 'yoghurt-weaving' (laughs).

As well as 'yoghurt weavers', who presented an image of squatting as an alternative and counter-cultural scene, Bryan and others also spoke of 'black underpants' anarchists who they characterised as steadfast and uncompromising when it came to engaging with anyone outside of the squats. When I asked Asher what defined black underpants anarchists, he laughed and replied:

Otherwise known as the 'anarcho-*cynical*ists'. Very cynical. Anarcho-cynicalists, very cynical. 'Neeeee ... talking to the council. Neeeee ... talking to the press. Neeeeee ... talking to academics. Neeeeeee!' (laughs)

Partly, the difficulty of public engagement with squats simply comes from being politically, culturally, and economically, marginalised. These overlap in diverse ways, reflecting different crews, buildings, circumstances, and political commitments around different campaigns and societal issues, which don't always lend themselves to being palatable to the 'public'. Yet, for Bryan, the whole point of having social centres in the first place was to create spaces to engage and connect with others:

The purpose of these communities, including squatting communities, is to make people feel empowered. It enables a self-organisation of homeless people and that's crucial. It keeps the pressure up. Because against us, against *the movement*, we've got the weight of capital ... and in a city like London, that is a terrifyingly huge weight and amount of financial and political power. Also of course, we've got this incredible decline of public space in a city like London. What you need is free spaces all the time.

Who a particular crew have in mind as 'the public' or 'the community' when they open a space is likely shaped by their location. For example, if they are located on or near to a housing estate threatened with regeneration, or a slowly gentrifying high street, the tendency is for anarchist/socialist squatters to connect with existing campaigns in the area. In these cases, social centres act as infrastructure on the neighbourhood level, perhaps providing meeting space, event space, networking space, or other resources. Alternatively, social centres can operate on wider transnational or existential scales, positioning themselves as spaces for 'radical' political campaigns to take necessary action on the climate crisis or to build campaigns against war or capitalism.

What these different scales shared in common, Bryan argued, was that they demonstrated how squatting a building is always a political action:

The most meaningful action on housing ... the most meaningful environmental action ... is you *stop something from happening*. You lock-on to the tractor. You lock-on to the digger ... You stop the power station from running for a day. And the most effective action in *housing* is to actually *make* housing. To house people. So any housing movement which doesn't have a squatting wing, which isn't looking seriously at how to occupy buildings, I'm not very interested in actually. I'm glad they exist, but they just sound like lobbyists to me. And I think their lobbying would be so much more effective if they had a powerful social movement behind them, taking direct action.

Here, Bryan is drawing parallels between squatters and environmental activists locking themselves to tractors and diggers to prevent road building or quarrying. Because squatting makes a physical intervention into city space, without waiting for permission from existing owners or authorities, it creates an immediate and direct political challenge:

Squatting has a very *immediate* role. OK, well we can only do commercial properties, but we just saw a fantastic example with Streets Kitchen. By doing that occupation, which they do in the teeth of the law and the police, and getting all the mainstream media so lots of people get to know about it ... they're saying: '*This* is what we need to be doing, all the time, automatically.' Without squatting, that doesn't happen.

INFOSHOPS

Perhaps the most renowned and long-standing infoshop in London is the Advisory Service for Squatters (ASS), who are currently located at the Freedom bookshop in Whitechapel, where they host practical squatter nights, share information and literature, and provide spaces for organising. I met Iker at the offices on the top floor. He had left school at 16 and got a 'fairly normal' job, but then started meeting people who were squatting and 'having what seemed like a better time and more constructive ... they were doing creative things and trying to change the world.' After working for four years, he 'retired' at 20 and became a full-time activist:

I decided that, you know, changing the world was not going to come from people who dropped out. It's going to come from 'ordinary people' ... although, I've never met an 'ordinary person' in my life! (laughs)

Initially, Iker was quite 'anti-squatter'. But while renting a bedsit, working for the Islington Unwaged Centre, and participating in the Labour movement, he met some squatters who had set up a social centre down the road:

We got on really well. We found we had almost everything in common. And one of them mentioned that they were looking for a new squat so I joined in with them. And we had a fantastic collective squat where it was ... we were doing loads of stuff together. We were involved in supporting the miners' strike and stuff like that.

Iker distinguished the 'mass squatting movement' in the 1970s from the 'new movement' that he was involved in during the 1980s, describing the latter as 'punks who came to London looking for freedom, which they didn't have in their little towns'. Under Thatcherism and mass unemployment, he characterised 'most of the punks I hung with' as 'hippies really, but they were more angry'. For Iker, the movements which were being sustained through squats had become less optimistic about change, but also increasingly expressed themselves through infoshops and social centres, which provided 'continuity':

> There was a big squat called the Peace Centre which was quite messy. But you know, lots of young people, mainly new to London, and it was people living there but also a drop-in and activist centre … vegan café, different meetings, squatting and other housing advice … if you weren't punky or anarcho, you probably would get funny looks if you went in. It wasn't outreach at all … it was *of* the movement, it wasn't outward-looking.

Frustrated, Iker dropped out of squatting again, but remained active in other campaigns such as the anti-Poll Tax campaign and unwaged movements. He only later got involved again, he tells me, because of a scheme to reduce unemployment, which provided an extra £10 a week for volunteers, and led him to work for ASS:

> I said: 'Right, I'm not doing anything else and I don't want to get involved in local activism, so I'll do that for six months and see what happens.' And six months must have ran out about … 24 years ago. (laughs)

At the time, ASS were based in Hackney where the council were closing down short-life housing cooperatives and encouraging people to move into tenancies. Iker got involved by opening up social centres in the borough, because 'all the people who had been in short-life co-ops or had been squatting and were now tenants, they were totally isolated and they wanted somewhere where they could get back together.'

As one of the longest lasting members of ASS, often working with and supporting squatters directly with legal cases and advice, Iker has clear insight into the wider squatting scene in London:

> It's a mix. I mean, for some in London, it's about people having space they can afford because space is unaffordable generally. It's also about challenging property relations, particularly the fact that people can own and keep empty property that people need … And it's, for *me* … it's the easiest expression of ordinary people taking the things that they need rather than waiting for them to be given to us or having to pay for them … this is people taking control of their own lives and the things that they need.

ASS doesn't take an explicit stance on whether squatters should or should not negotiate in order to hold on to spaces. Instead, they stick to giving legal advice and allow people to make their own decisions: 'if people say they want to negotiate, we'll always suggest ways of doing it ... but yeah, if people don't want to, then that's fine.' Personally, though, Iker is 'on the negotiation side':

> When I started, you didn't even need to [negotiate] you know? I didn't bother going to court. I didn't do any of the things that ASS says you should do because I could just move on. You know, we'd be looking for somewhere else and we'd be moving on when courts came. And you had long enough. Since then, I'd say, negotiating works ... I guess the difference between here and places like Germany and Holland, where people did have to fight ... but in a way, fighting is a *form* of negotiation ...

Context is key. After squatting in residential buildings was made more difficult, Iker tells me there was, at first, a massive reduction of people turning to squatting, particularly with the rise of guardianships. From his perspective, squatting was now 'mainly done by people who are activists or part of the scene, *or* quietly by people who probably don't even know about ASS ... you know?' While he had been drawn back into squatting because 'it was easy for anybody to do ... you just go out and do it', he also added that 'it's not like that now':

> And I can see that, you know, there are people who want to push for a more hardline position. People should fight more. [But] I'm still up for negotiating and ASS helping with negotiating if necessary.

The question of whether to negotiate is tricky. On the one hand, squatters have perhaps been forced to be less 'hard-line' on negotiation and more likely to seek out compromise so they might continue using space in an insecure and precarious city. Yet there is simultaneously an ongoing need for free and 'public' spaces where communities can come together, which can be limited by bringing ownership into the space. Formalisation brings possible restrictions and new challenges, such as paying the rent or organising the space under the scrutiny of private owners or the state, who are now empowered to withdraw their leniency at short notice. Formalisation, however, provides longevity, which means squats can take on the role of dependable nodes in the wider campaign networks, as well as semi-secure spaces for sustaining community by providing resources such as space, time, and information.

The 56a Infoshop is on the other side of the river from ASS, south of Elephant and Castle. In the context of widespread regeneration in the area, their juxtaposition with the new-build flats on the opposite side of the street represents a microcosm of social struggles in Southwark. At the front is the 'Fareshares' food cooperative, selling fruit and vegetables off tables which can be easily pushed aside for the meetings and workshops regularly held here. At the back, the bookshop is full of zines, pamphlets, leaflets, and posters for various protests, days of action, marches, and campaigns, as well as adverts for practical squatter nights and crews looking for people to join them. This is also where you will find the impressive 56a archive: shelves of binders and boxes filled with various materials from decades of squatting and activism across south London, the UK, and beyond. On just one shelf, the boxes read from left to right: 'Radical Southwark Festival Oct'98'; 'Southwark Radical Histories – Notes, Pamphlets, Cuttings, Hints'; 'Radical History South London: Lambeth, Wandsworth …'; 'Class Theory: Pamphlets, Leaflets'; 'Radical History London: Central London, General London Riots, North East London'; 'Radical History London: East End, West London, Notting Hill, North London'; 'Radical History: Bristol, Luton, Manchester, Newcastle'. The shelf below was labelled 'Art & Politics – Criticism, History, Class, Provocations, Bullshit'.

The 56a Infoshop had initially been squatted in 1988 but it took three years for Southwark Council to notice. As Carson tells the story, the squatters were eventually taken to court in 1991, but they were already trying to negotiate with the council to keep using the building:

Look, why don't we try to come to some arrangement? Don't go ahead with possession. We'll come to some arrangement. The council were like: 'okay, that's fine, we'll be in touch'. They didn't get in touch for 12 years (laughs).

In 2003, the future of the space was put in jeopardy, when someone at Southwark Council noticed that no one was paying rent on the property:

They were like 'Oh, what's going on here?' They pretty much said at the time 'The problem we have is you're flagged up as not paying rent, why don't you pay … let's make an arrangement and you pay rent.' So, you know, in good sense [the crew] maintained the project. The [council] bureaucrat quite liked the project because it was out of the hands of any political department: it was pure property services. He basically said: 'Someone's looking over my back, they're going [to ask] why is there no rent from that property?' So, we formalised to become tenants.

The squatters agreed a formal arrangement with the council. While only paying a 'peppercorn' rent, however, they were now exposed to potential rent increases in the future, or their agreement being potentially withdrawn by the council if they caused too many problems. What's more, as part of their compromise with the council, they also had to give up part of the building they had squatted:

When they formalised everything, they actually evicted us [from part of the building] so we lost a lot of space. We had a huge bike workshop at the bottom. But that was fine, we just lost it. But it's a funny place, isn't it? Because it's just *maintained* itself. It's just kept going. Who knows, we may be affected by the gentrification at some point.

Yet for Carson, compromise also meant they could be a constant in a wider precarious and insecure network of squats. They could offer dependable space for gatherings, meetings, and workshops, where people could come together and connect, but also for hosting a vast and accessible archive, acting as a historical and authoritative location for collective belonging and identity. Despite having to take on new considerations, such as how to raise and manage money, for them the value of the space continued to be its use:

[After negotiation] those kind of legal spaces are *essentially* the same, but less messy. It's very *practical* to run them. You have to raise money. You have to have committees to do this. You have to think through all sorts of stuff. But in some ways, they're a continuation. We need space and space is what makes thinking through social relations [possible] ... [you can] imagine with freedom what you can do and what you can't do (always with tensions of course).

Carson made regular comparisons between 56a and the 121 Centre in Brixton, itself a significant bricks-and-mortar entry into London's great archive of squats. 121 Railton Road had originally been squatted by Black Panther activists Olive Morris and Liz Obi in the early 1970s and was the first squat of a privately owned building in Brixton. One eviction attempt was immortalised on the cover of the 1979 edition of the *Squatters Handbook*, showing Morris climbing up onto the roof of 121 and waiting for the police to leave. 121 then became the Sabaar bookshop and was used as a centre for the Brixton Black Panther Movement as well as the Black Advice Centre. While not the first black bookshop in Brixton, it survived the Unity bookshop, which was destroyed by a firebomb in 1973. As an infoshop, Sabaar is an example of squatting establishing the spaces people need in defiance of a city that sought to deny them that space.[19] As well as demonstrating that 'we shall not be terrorised out of existence', such spaces also supported important publications, which 'paved the way for stronger forms of black literary self-expression in the form of poetry and the novel'.[20]

Just before the Brixton Uprising in 1981, Sabaar bookshop accepted council funding for new premises (later becoming the Black Cultural Archives)[21] and the squat became an anarchist infoshop – the 121 Centre – until 1999. 'I was in and out of involvement with that space' Carson told me:

> The first time I ever went to Brixton was when I was still at A-level college and me and my mate went in ... It was very typically a kind of anar-cho-syndicalist flavoured squat. And of course, we were very young and we didn't know much about histories of anarchism ... but it was like a home you know? You were like: 'Oh, this is great!' So, we picked up some free stuff. We'd come back with copies of *Crowbar* magazine ...

During the Brixton Uprising 1981, while 'tonnes of stuff was fucked up' on Railton Road, the infoshop 'wasn't touched'. One theory was because there was a poster in the window expressing solidarity with the 'riots' in St Pauls, Bristol, which had happened the year before. Yet Carson points out that it's unclear what the relationship was like between the 121 Centre and Brixton's black community – 'there was no real crossover, I don't think ... there were very few local black people involved.' Mostly, the campaigns associated with the squat from the early 1980s onwards were not *explicitly* anti-racist cam-paigns, instead leaning more towards the gender and sexuality politics of the squats on Vauxhall Road – including Queeruption festival, as well as *Bad Attitude* and *Shocking Pink* magazines, as well as environmentalist and peace movements – suggesting that this centre was ultimately *unsuccessful* in terms of engaging with the community around it.

SQUATTING AS A MEANS

Some of the squatters I have met in London seemed to take a much more instrumental approach to the practice of occupying empty spaces for ongoing use. For them, squats are just one tool in a wider activist repertoire, a useful means for supporting *other* campaigns that are not necessarily associated specifically with squats and squatting. Nico, Raleigh, and Tig all claimed that the fact that a place was a *squatted* space was incidental, and that their engagement with social centres only came through their prior engagement with social movements. But it became clear through our conversation that, for all three, squatting had become crucial as a way to stay located and free up time in London, so they could continue to contribute to various campaigns.

'I suppose it was Occupy London when I first met a lot of squatters,' Nico recalled, 'and subsequently ... Occupy London sort of moved into lots of different squats.' Beginning in London in October 2011, one month after the first Occupy protest in New York as part of the 'Arab Spring, European Summer, and American Fall' of that year, the most high-profile Occupy camp in London had been outside St Paul's Cathedral. But the movement had also occupied other spaces across the city, some of which persisted after the eviction at St Paul's in February 2012:

> After the Bank of Ideas, after Finsbury Square, and after St Paul's was evicted, the very last bastion was this place called the Hobo Hilton. It was in Holborn and it was a *huge* building, probably about six storeys. It was the biggest squat I think I've ever seen. There were lots and lots of students there, lots of homeless, they opened the door to anyone. The door was just pretty much open ... yeah, some criminally insane people in that building (laughs).

Raleigh had also been involved with Occupy (in) London, but her first experiences with squatting had come much earlier when she was 18 and a young mother: 'It was a way to get housing when I needed housing *and* it was a way to be part of a community when I was a single parent.' But Raleigh had only become aware of squatting through her involvement with the free festival scene as a teenager:

> At that time, [mainstream] culture I think felt to me ... I suppose it was now what I would call 'capitalism'. Quite an alienating culture. [But] that

free festival movement was a bit more about 'do it yourself'. We could make *our own* music. We could make *our own* parties. It was sort of cultural rejection, to me, of the sort of 'corporate world'. Although I wouldn't have phrased it [that way] at that time (laughs).

Looking back, she realised that her involvement in free festivals was political, but at the time had not framed it in this way. Her turn to squatting was driven by needing a supportive community, but also the DIY ethos which she already valued:

I don't think I felt particularly secure and stable when squatting. But then I formed a cooperative with my neighbours, and I still live in that house, and it's still a cooperative. And then we joined with other cooperatives. So, we sort of *regularised* our houses and we put a lot of work into that. I mean, I personally rewired my house with friends, and put in toilets. We really invested in our houses and in our communities. And we negotiated over the long-term with the councils for short-term lets and now it's permanent. Now I view that as a sort of *commons* really.

The chance to participate was also what first attracted Tig in 2008/9 when he attended a punk gig at a squatted ice-cream shop. Similarly to Raleigh, however, there were other reasons why Tig first got involved. Having rented for years and worked as an English teacher, he was massively in debt with no money for a deposit, and began 'overstaying' on people's sofas. It was a practical squatters night at 56a which got him into squatting:

I met a guy ... ex-military, queer. He was sleeping illegally in the hotel he was working in ... sleeping on the bus some nights. We decided we were going to go out and start trying to find a place to live.

With Nico, Raleigh, and Tig, it's difficult (and perhaps pointless) to try and disentangle whether they were motivated by the politics of squatting, whether they were already into the politics which they led them to squatting, or whether they were driven by their housing situation. What becomes clear, with Tig for instance, is that once he got into squatting he began to understand his own circumstances in more explicitly political terms: drawing connections between his own life and wider public issues.

After a few years, Tig took a break from squatting, before coming back a few years later to join a squat in Hackney:

That was a very consciously, overtly political occupation. Number one: I needed a place to live. But I had these ideas, and I began to see how that could be enacted with groups. I met people who were practising sort of, overtly political ideas and relationships.

After Hackney, Tig went on to help set up and run other social centres across London, with the aim of establishing spaces that could be used by various local communities and/or different campaign groups. Similarly, Nico had also got involved in multiple social centres after Occupy, including The Hive in Dalston, which he described as having struggled with their public image:

At the moment, they're still being portrayed a bit of a 'squat'. It sounds a bit obvious, but they still look like 'we're a load of hippies'. They've got like hippie graffiti on the side of the building and people look at it and think 'Ah, it's *that*.' I'm not saying that the hippie thing is bad, but you know ... if you put graffiti on a building, they'd be like 'Ah, that's a criminal building for criminals.'

From Nico's perspective, using squatting as a means also meant potentially becoming part of the 'squatting scene', which risked compromising any goals of engaging with publics and campaigning around wider issues. There was a heavy reliance on different 'types' of squats in his account and, in particular, he drew a distinction between 'political' and 'non-political' squatting. On the one hand, 'non-political' squats were 'very, very tight-knit ... they're only letting their close friends in and people that can be trusted', which made them potentially exclusive. Yet what he called 'the political' squats 'to a certain degree ... don't mind letting everyone in, you know?' which created its own set of issues:

A lot of squatters are, shall we say, disenfranchised youth, and like a bit, shall we say, unhappy with the current status quo and the government, you know? They're going to rebel against the system at protests and stuff like that. They're also going to rebel in the sort of way of taking drugs and, you know, alcohol abuse and all that. So, you know, you find yourself in spots where everyone's on a completely different ... some people are pissed, some people are stoned, some people are on, you know, whatever you call them, like downers and everyone's on their own buzz. And this is going to cause ... you know, this is a boiling pot.

In contrast, Nico distinguished his *own* involvement with various protest camps and squats during the Occupy movement in London as having provided a valuable political space:

A space to breathe and a space to actually operate and get organised. Occupy *was* that space. When you're sitting together with people, when you're knocking heads together and actually talking things out, you can get so much more done. I think, back in the day, when there was ten thousand plus squats in the centre of London, there was bit more of a code of conduct and people had a bit more *respect* ... it didn't feel like you were living on the edge and you were going to get evicted tomorrow.

While Nico eventually decided to just 'get out of squatting' altogether, Raleigh insisted that she had found a route to escaping the precarity of squatting while still holding on to the politics which had attracted her in the first place, when her crew decided to formalise as a housing cooperative. Not only did this mean that they could now access grants for bigger repair jobs (such as fixing the roof) which was 'beyond our sort of DIY skills', but they also, at least in the short term, had some security against eviction. Actually living in the cooperative, however, had its own difficulties:

It is challenging to sort of live democratically and to sort of run things collaboratively ... I think we live in a society which is sort of quite hierarchical, there's a deference to experts, *and* there's not necessarily a culture of people getting involved in things or feeling able to get involved in things ... I think those are the two challenges really to sort of running a *commons*. The ability for people to step up, and feel able to take responsibility, and feel *empowered* to take responsibility.

Again, like Nico, Raleigh also compared her experience in the cooperative with Occupy (in) London:

In Occupy, people did step up and get involved and sort of discover themselves. I mean, I certainly had the experience of discovering all these different things I could do ... There's a really exciting energy, I think, that happens initially with Occupy and free festivals and stuff like that. Then you do get some of the organising challenges ...

Whether it was squatting, Occupy, or cooperatives, the problem for Raleigh really came down to relations of *property*. At Occupy (in) London, she had been involved in developing a safer spaces policy, based on a restorative justice model which sought to 'deal with difficult behaviour' and 'mediate some conflicts'. In her words, they 'did have quite a lot of homeless people or people sort of *on the edge* who came ...' some who 'really became integrated in Occupy', but others 'a little bit less so'. For Raleigh, the question was how best to manage their 'boundaries':

> Because you can't hold your boundaries in open space. I think that is a learning from Occupy. So, when we did Occupy Democracy, it was *thoughtfully* done. It was going to be ten days, and it was going to be 'in' and it was going to be 'out'. Giving ten days was a boundary.

By demarcating the use of space at Occupy Democracy – a follow-up protest which took over the green outside the Houses of Parliament in 2014 – the intention was still to use occupation in order to support a political campaign, but one which was less susceptible to being undermined by occupation as a means.

While never referring to 'boundaries', Tig also picked up on similar diffi-culties of organising spaces:

> I did come back in 2013 and I found my old crew and they were living in a big place in Chalk Farm with like 30 people. The building actually almost divided up floor by floor, from like 'politically conscious' squatters on the top (if I can call them that), migrants and workers in the middle, and then drugs and party-time on the ground floor (laughs). We had this real structure, potentially hierarchy, physically manifest. I don't think it was conscious, but the three floors worked really nicely. Each floor had a kitchen, so each group within it could kind of self-organise a little bit more ... it was still connected. It's kind of one of the most ideal buildings I'd lived in I'd say.

However, after they were evicted, 'now the dilemma of we're looking for a building for 30 people'. Divisions within the squat flared under the stress of finding a new space. Some of those who considered themselves to be more politically conscious than others began to split into smaller and smaller crews 'because they'd been so hardline on "this is the way that we do things"'. The crew at Chalk Farm eventually moved into an old police station which 'the individualists fucking loved ... because they took over the cells'. But the division created by the layout of the building caused tensions in itself, including 'huge disagreements between the very overtly political collectivists and then the individualists within it ... you end up with a 15-hour house meeting and then of course that building gets evicted anyway and there's *another* split':

> There becomes increasing stress in terms of people's capacity and ability to organise and make things happen. For me, it kind of got to a point where I would rather just go and do *something* than go through another meeting about what to do.

Tig tells me that, under the pressure, he began to 'abuse amphetamine in order to keep going':

> Because it was like you're running and running and running at this level that the environment *generates* drug abuse, not the other way round. When we had stable places, our habits were under control. It's when you're living in this kind of situation, that's when it starts to escalate.

Together, Nico, Raleigh, and Tig all had routes into squatting which were far from one-dimensional. While they may, at first, appear to have been driven by their pre-involvement in existing movements and subcultures, their continued involvement in various spaces suggests that there was more to the story. Squatting was never simply a 'means'. For all three – at various points in their lives and with different crews and buildings – motivations constantly moved between housing need, community belonging, locational needs, and political aspirations. What's more, while they had experiences in various occupied spaces that sought to establish themselves as explicitly 'political', they also found it difficult in practice to organise these spaces towards clear campaigns and political ends. Tig was particularly bitter about his experiences with various crews and the way in which people appeared ready to abandon collective projects and split into different 'types' so easily. Despite making repeated references to different types of squats and squatters in our interview, he was clear on what he thought of 'types' in practice:

> It's *bullshit*. It's just a way to split, that's it, just a tactic to divide. In my experience, I have fallen into both ... so it's like 'Oh, that's a drug addict squat' or 'That's like a ...' It's just carving divisions between people who

are ostensibly in solidarity with each other in terms of self-directing their housing in London. Hair-splitting serves a very specific purpose which is to prevent the idea of a collective identity.

SQUATTING AS DIRECT ACTION

Separated by 25 years, Grow Heathrow and Claremont Road both represent campaigns against state-led infrastructural projects which have used squatting as direct environmental action. While the former was an occupation in the far west of the city to prevent the building of a third runway at Heathrow Airport, the latter was a street which had been emptied to make way for the M11 link road in north-east London. On one side, Frosty had got heavily involved in Grow Heathrow in order to push back against the expansion of air travel. And on the other, Emin had been heavily involved at Claremont Road as part of the wider anti-roads campaigns of the early 1990s. Both framed their protests in these spaces in terms of the global and existential threat of the climate emergency. Both are also clear examples of squatting being used as direct action by getting in the way of proposed projects.

'They say it was the biggest road-building scheme since the Romans' Emin remembered:

It was Margaret Thatcher, £23billion worth of new roads scheme, trashing so many different places, orbitals, you name it you know. That was her way of feeding into the car culture.

After just about making it to the infamous Twyford Down protests, Emin was a budding filmmaker, searching for the 'next big protest to cover' as well as somewhere to live, just as the campaign against the M11 link road kicked off in Walthamstow, London. All along the planned route of the new road were rows of vacant houses that had been emptied using compulsory purchase orders. Some now had artists staying in them on 'meanwhile' leases, but 'in general, most of the streets were just abandoned':

Entire streets boarded-up. Waiting for demolition. So, we just moved in and, well, *initially* I was making a documentary. But it's blurry because it was the birth of video activism. So, it's kind of like, you are an *activist*, but you're also on that other side of the *media-type* side, you know?

When the call for support to fight the M11 link road went out, Emin said that people had travelled from protests at Twyford Down, Jesmond Dene, Stamworth Valley, and Salisbury Hill, as well as 'tribal people' – such as Flowerpot Tribe, Rainbow Tribe, Dongas – who would travel between different protests and free festivals. 'That was pretty much most of the '90s really', Emin explained, 'a lot of travelling, a lot of occupying, a lot of moving on … well, getting moved on.' Squats were set up all along the proposed route of the M11 link road, including the 'Free Independent Republic of Wanstonia' and a tree on George's Green (which, apparently, was the first tree to be registered as a legal dwelling in the UK). While Emin did include all of these in his documentary, however, his main focus was the row of houses on Claremont Road:

> I just got into barricading. I got into campaigning full time. I did a little bit of camera work, but I got more and more into the actual idea of 'taking and protecting', you know, *defending* a bit of land or a house against eviction.

Aspiring towards a more sustainable future that wasn't reliant on car travel and fossil fuels, Claremont Road aimed to take direct action on the road-building programme and environmental destruction. At the time, climate change was 'still pretty much seen as a bogus science … like "tin hat brigade" kind of concept', but following the United Nations Rio Earth Summit in 1992, activists began to use squatted social centres and info-centres both to educate themselves and spread information on different campaigns:

> Cool Tan Arts, Brixton. I used to go there. That's how I found out about Twyford Down. Convinced some guy to drive us down there, you know. You can find out through leaflets or benefits [fundraisers] or something … You find out an issue and you get behind it. Find out when the march was.

Squats were also spaces where tactics, strategies, and experiences of occupations were shared. For Emin, there was a clear sea-change in London's squatting scene in the early 1990s, even if the tactic of taking and holding buildings was the same:

> Squatting became a kind of *tactic in itself* to slow up the road building, you know? It shifted a gear. It was more *proactive* in the sense that, you know, whereas squatters might want to keep their head down in some situations,

and just 'live', and just get on with it, and not create too much attention to themselves ... the kind of squatting that we were doing in the '90s: we were *deliberately* taking property. Deliberately looking like we were going to resist the bailiffs and building up a kind of momentum of resistance. Making it as difficult as possible for them to get us out. Through lock-ons, through tunnels, even towers.

Emin showed me some photographs of the infrastructure they created at Claremont Road (which has become the stuff of activist legend). Trenches. Lock-on barrels. Cargo net walkways between trees and buildings. Burnt-out cars filled with rubble, blocking the road, but which had been decorated as if they were an art installation on the street: 'Art as a necessity, art as a strategy, you know?' said Emin, laughing at a slogan spraypainted on one of the cars: 'rust in peace'. Perhaps the most iconic instalment was the scaffolding tower which had been created to make it as unsafe as possible for bailiffs to remove people from the top. But Emin's *pièce de résistance* was the 'rat run' – a tunnel across the first floor of seven terraced houses and barricaded on the floor below with the stairs removed. For good measure, sheets of tin had also been added beneath the roof tiles and barbed wire in the walls. When the eviction finally came, Emin tells me, it was the most expensive in UK history: 'Seventy-three hours and it cost £2.3 million and a thousand police.'

For Emin, the importance of squatting was in providing a space to congregate, to come together, converge, and act in common. In particular, he had in mind the 491 Gallery, a squatted social centre and art exhibition/studio space, which he saw as fulfilling a specific social need before it was evicted:

We got some criticism from the wider squatting community, but we did hold it together and we had a lot of important events which we managed to do for the 491 for about 10 years. Fundraisers and sort-of gigs. Car-free days we organised. A lot of stuff from, say, in 2003 all that [protest against the] war against Iraq stuff came out of the 491 ... There's potentially community hubs all over the place ... with accommodation upstairs ... I mean Claremont. That was like barricading houses, that was covering windows, ripping out stairs, making it expensive to evict us and ... [time-consuming] and costly, you know. 491 was the opposite. It was putting in windows, fixing floors, fixing stairs, you know. And I much prefer that side of it you know. Just creating *something out of nothing*.

There are many similarities between Claremont Road and Grow Heathrow, but they also differ: Claremont was more *destructive* in their direct action (as part of the barricading); while Grow Heathrow was intended to be more *creative* and 'prefigurative' (i.e. aiming to *be* and *live* the change they wanted to see in the world). Frosty had initially trained to be an architect for five years and had been working in an architect's office when he became frustrated with the stress of the job. 'I needed a big change', he recalled, 'and I had in mind to move to do something more radical and more political.' After attending a party at Grow Heathrow, he realised that he could go and live there, and ended up staying for almost four years:

> So, I kind of went down there. I don't know ... because I really supported their main issue, their main cause, really to try and block the expansion of Heathrow Airport. Their party scene ... seemed like a good time to go there, met loads of lovely people.

The squatted garden centre had formerly been a supplier of fruit and vegetables to market stalls in London before the business was made commercially unviable by cheaper overseas imports. After shutting down, the site had remained derelict, but had somehow survived plans by the landlord to develop it into an airport car park in the 1990s. When it was first squatted, the original aspiration was to do more than just put themselves in the way of a third runway, it was also to 'take that bit of space and turn it into a community garden, so that it could be used by the community':

> And so, for me, that was the big appeal of it. It's like creating a positive thing in a negative situation. Taking something that's, you know, *en route* to either becoming an airport or a car park for the airport, or you keep it as what it is: a green space. And you give the community access to it. They can grow their own vegetables there. And at the same time, people can live there, totally off-grid as well. So that was the vision.

While Frosty was living there, he slept in what he described as 'a glorified shed with insulation and a wood-burner'. Now living on a boat, he told me this was definitely a good step up, yet was quick to add that he learnt many of the skills he needed to live off-grid while he was squatting, including woodwork, solar panels, and maintaining a compost toilet. Describing himself as 'middle class', Frosty never felt he was in a position where he had no choice but to squat, but one of the things that first attracted him to Grow Heathrow had been the diversity of people who rotated through the space:

> We were trying to provide a space that was open to all really. Because, you know, we didn't *own* it, and we didn't think anyone should own it, so therefore anyone is welcome to come and stay there. And yeah ... you got a real mixture of people and that's what I loved about it. And then, you know, people come from different backgrounds I guess there's going to be conflicts of worldviews and just different ways of approaching things. And I think there were certainly people who, although they weren't going to be homeless if they moved out, were in a very precarious situation ... Then there is a kind of conflict, but it just is difficult ... I think some people really wanted the project to be focused on stopping the expansion of Heathrow Airport and the local community.

This connection with the 'local community' was important for Frosty, both in terms of the anti-ownership politics of squatting and their aim of opening up an enclosed and disused space. But it was also important for the environmental politics of Grow Heathrow and spreading their wider campaign against expanding air travel and the use of fossil fuels:

> The kind of idea is that you create a really strong relationship with the local community and they support you, *that* is your best defence against being evicted. And at the same time, it's a great way to live and to be part of a thriving community. You'll then hopefully be effective in holding that space and stopping the airport from expanding, you know?

There had been some conflicts with the neighbours, particularly around late-night music and smoke from the wood-burners getting onto clothes which had been hung out to dry. But on the whole, it seemed that those living in nearby houses saw their own fate as tied in with the protest (given that their homes would be flattened by the runway as well). The squatters, at least at the beginning, made active efforts to build connections with the neighbours by opening up the main gate every day for visitors and encouraging people not to smoke weed around visiting children:

> So, you know, it was always really strict about 'That's not the thing we do during the day.' People can [smoke] on the weekend, or whatever, and no one's going to stop you then. But it's inappropriate for a space which

is trying to be open to the public and that kind of thing. There is drugs and that in [squatting] culture. But my experience was that people were able to indulge in those drugs and then also be really fucking on it when they're not on drugs, if you know what I mean. While I was there, it didn't become a drug den.

Like Emin, Frosty saw the importance of squatting as being part of wider networks, campaigns, and solidarities which could be sustained through them, but he also saw this as creating a potential problem in terms of spreading important messages and building 'public' momentum around an issue:

Potentially, you're kind of creating tribes, which is great when you're in it and you're part of this strong family, you know? But then I think the thing about that is that you can get other people outside of that who you can't relate to them so well and they can't relate to you. And that's an issue. I think if you're trying to make what you're doing something that actually 'takes off', you know, on a large scale that isn't just for you ...

For both Grow Heathrow and Claremont Road, the means of protest (squatting) was simultaneously the ends, in that their wider campaigns and aspirations for a sustainable future relied on their successful occupation of their particular location. The Grow Heathrow squatters were fighting eviction through the court system, making a moral argument that they were putting disused space – which Frosty described as 'being *abused* by the landowners' – to a higher and better use as creative space. 'We actually improved it for the local community', Frosty pointed out, 'so the local council were like "Oh yeah, fair enough, this is fine with us."' Whereas, for the squatters in Claremont Road, their 'deconstruction' of the houses to make their eviction more difficult was successful in drawing massive public attention to the impact the road-building programme would have through destroying the natural environment. Although the M11 link road was eventually built, the anti-roads protests were successful in the long run, with the road programme scrapped by 1997.

THE ENDS AND THE MEANS

People can have different aspirations for the same space – whether a building, a neighbourhood, or a planet – and the messiness and tension that ensues is a property relationship. In squats, however, this is not automatically shut down through the ownership model. Instead, squatters have the opportunity to embrace the complexity, partly because they do not carry the authority of ownership to call upon the state to help them exclude users they see as illegitimate, but also because many want to find ways of facilitating diversity, inclusion, and empowerment. Whether a particular squat can be used for multiple purposes depends on the vision that people have in that squat. Some might just want to keep their head down in a particular building, while others might have ambitions to open the space to the public as part of their wider politics surrounding empty buildings (e.g. re-opening a library) and/or creating spaces for wider social change.

The examples shared here show varied attempts to use squatting to create spaces and networks for wider social change. Squatted spaces provide physical and social flexibility where different campaigns, perspectives, and experiences can clash, as well as valuable infrastructure for voices that are otherwise being marginalised. There can be limits to using squatted spaces for this purpose, however. In the context of wider stigma, public relations can be hard to manage and it can be difficult to engage local communities. There is a danger that even squats that set themselves up as 'social centres' or 'infoshops' become isolated: perceived as subcultural enclaves rather than open spaces for democratic engagement and participation. Squats are crucial infrastructure for marginalised communities to converge and connect, but they are also campaign spaces which attempt to engage wider publics on the politics of marginalisation. This can be contradictory, because the very means by which they have been able to create infrastructure (squatting) carries with it the stigmas and stereotypes which can scupper public engagement. This can also create struggles within squats between those trying to maintain some sort of welcoming and inviting public image when opening up spaces, with the aim of gaining momentum behind their campaign(s); versus the use of squats as private, domestic, 'safety nets below the safety net', that can provide refuge, care, solidarity, and mutual support.

Squats can also struggle to hold on to a location for long enough to build relationships and trust with neighbours from which participation could stem. Non-squatted or formerly squatted space, where the crew have negotiated with the state or a private owner, can therefore be vital for maintaining some sort of longevity and reliability. Sometimes, local authorities (most notably in Amsterdam, Copenhagen, and Paris) have even sought to actively *tolerate* squatted social centres, allowing them to continue using a building as a youth centre or artist space, while forcing them to take on a 'meanwhile' agreement. Such schemes have been criticised for creating a 'two-tier' system, between 'good' squatters (who are turned into legitimate users of city space allowed to stay, such as artists) and 'bad' squatters (who are not offered a deal and are then evicted).[22] Many squatters therefore are 'hard-line' and refuse to negotiate as a matter of principle, which can lead to a drawn-out eviction battle in the courts and/or on the street. Once again, even in non-squatted or formerly squatted spaces, we see the potential problem of the means corrupting the ends, insofar as a formal agreement might place conditions on the kind of politics which can be expressed or materially embodied in the space, as 'radical ideas are twisted, commodified and absorbed into a more institutionally acceptable context'.[23] The risk is not only that squats become pacified and incorporated into marketised narratives around cool and edgy 'creative cities', but that they might become the shock troops for gentrification.[24]

On the one hand, then, negotiated spaces provide (some) longevity and stability for the network in a volatile context. Yet negotiation can create even more challenges by bringing in elements of the ownership model (e.g. contracts, rent, bills), as well as limitations on what aspirations can be supported by the space (e.g. what the landlord or local authority will or will not allow you to do with the space). Make too many unauthorised changes to the layout or aesthetic of the building and there may be consequences from the legal owner (paying for 'damage' or a swift eviction). Be too radical and loud, and there is a risk of bringing unwanted attention to the space from the owner or harmful publics that may wish to attack or destroy the space. Yet be too quiet and it becomes difficult to spread information, campaign, and engage with publics outside of the squat.

In *The Squatters' Movement in Europe: Commons and Autonomy as Alternatives to Capitalism*, Cattaneo and Martinez argue that a squat 'can be intended either as a means towards something else … or as an end [in itself]'.[25] On the one hand, they identify 'necessity' squatting – where 'there is often no other motivation than to remedy a desperate situation, secretly and in silence' – but see this as having 'little to do with what is usually called political squatting', which 'offers a broader rationale for going beyond material housing need … [aiming] to prefigure ways of living beyond capitalist society'.[26] And yet they also recognise that separating 'social' and 'political' squatting is an extremely simplistic classification as 'any form of squatting is both'.[27] In isolation, necessity squatting might be considered as a way 'to have an available, cheap or free space … a mere resource', but 'obviously for some squatters the occupation itself is sufficiently anti-capitalist, because it challenges the plans and actions of capitalists over the built environment'.[28]

Separating the means and ends of squatting is, ultimately, *artificial*. As González, Diáz-Parra and Martínez-López have argued, 'squatting is simultaneously means and ends; squats serve to criticise urban speculation, institutional bureaucracy and the commodification of lives by capitalism, as much as they offer a direct solution (or spatial resource) for activists and sympathisers'.[29] Because squatting claims space, time, and location *in context*, the means and the politics *always* intersect. Even for those who appear to have at first started squatting from involvement in social movements or subcultures, we soon find that they have overlapping reasons for getting involved.

In other words, all squatting is direct action, even if the political significance isn't on the surface. Using an example borrowed by Norwegian Anarchist Syndicalist Beyer-Arensen, David Graeber offers a specific definition of what counts as 'direct action' (a term often banded around without much thought to its meaning):

> Imagine a town that suffers from a lack of water. Some real estate magnate owns all the surrounding land and has the mayor in his pocket, so townsfolk cannot simply build new wells. If one were to assemble a group of townsfolk to dig a new well *anyway*, in defiance of the law, then that would be direct action. But if one were to have them blockade the mayor's house until he changed his policy, that would certainly not be. It might be far more militant than writing petitions or letters or lobbying; but it's just another version of the same thing: an appeal to the powers-that-be to change their behaviour. *It still recognises the authority a real direct action-ist would reject* ... The community that defies the law by building its own well is not simply acting for themselves; they are also setting an example of self-organisation to other communities.[30]

What's at stake with this provocation is more than academic. This is central to how we interpret and recognise non-institutional politics, as well as the importance of the relationship between an action and its context. Here, the collective (townsfolk) reject formal engagement with systems of government, but also the authority of the ownership model which 'prevents' them from simply acting (digging a well themselves). By taking that defiant action *anyway* (digging their own well), they simultaneously avoid engaging with these wider formal systems and create a campaign (an example which can be replicated by others). Similarly, squatting – in the *context* of the ownership model and regardless of the mix of circumstances and aspirations of a particular crew – is an example of 'digging your own well'. The aim is to directly shape the environment around you *in spite of* those powers that would prevent you from doing so, and potentially to do this in a way that speaks to wider political aspirations that go with and beyond a particular space and location. The means and the ends become the same.

Temporarily in Charlton

Figure 35 'I'm swearing at the city ... the general direction of Canary Wharf'
(Charlton, 2018)

Source: Photo by a participant.

It was the day before Temporary Autonomous Art (TAA) 2018 and I was
following the map on my phone from Charlton station: down the hill, over
two main roads, past an enormous supermarket distribution centre and
an industrial estate. Having been evicted from their first venue – a former
National Grid depot in Bow – the back-up building was a former headquarters for the bookmakers E. Coomes Ltd. Subsumed by a larger company in
2011, this office block had been unused ever since, vacantly overlooking
the Thames Barrier – those ten steel gates that protect London from being
overcome by the rising tide.

I had arranged to meet Quinn at the gate and she pushed it just wide
enough for me to duck under the padlocked chain. The corridors and stair-
wells inside were already full of people painting and stencilling. On each
floor, what had previously been rows of dusty offices were being transformed
into art installations, as well as spaces for talks, screenings, performances,
and a bar. On the roof, there were more artists hard at work. 'It was pretty
amazing to be on the side of the Thames like that,' Quinn reflected later:

Figure 36 'There is loads of space [in London], but we're not allowed to have it' (Charlton, 2018)

Source: Photo by a participant.

Probably, in a few years, that's just going to be high-rise flats or something no doubt. I think it was just funny to be on a roof where you could see all of this. When I go to *those* parts of the city [e.g. Canary Wharf], it just feels really weird and pristine and soulless. And obviously it's all about money. It's just like the city is centred around *them* and there's no place or other people to have their dreams happen as well. It's just like the only way you can survive in London – or the only way they want you to survive – is to play into this wider thing of the bankers and the city workers ... the creative elites ... everyone else should just work in the service industry.'

They had arrived in the early hours of the morning and 'started cleaning as soon as we got in because we were buzzing off the adrenaline!'

Just like 'Oh my god, we've got a building! We've actually managed to get another one!' So, we're just wide awake. We went onto the roof and watched the sunrise and were like 'Oh my god, this place is incredible!'

There had been some disagreement, however, about whether they could legitimately use the new building. Most of the block was clearly abandoned, with stacks of old computers, pictures from horse races, and ancient betting

Figure 37   Temporary Autonomous Art (Charlton, 2018)
Source: Photo by the author.

machines. Shortly after getting inside, though, they found an office which still had signs of being used, including a laptop and a fridge which contained food still in date. There was a discussion about whether they should find somewhere else but, in the end, they agreed to simply seal off that room in an attempt to protect the belongings. Quinn told me this wasn't the first TAA where they'd had to do something like this. Once, they managed to negotiate with a landlord to stay for the weekend, so long as they promised to protect a sports car which was being stored on the premises.

The organisers had blocked off the third floor as 'Crew Only', so they had somewhere separate to sleep and cook. 'We usually just make it a mission to make loads of food,' explained Quinn:

Food is really good just for getting people to sit down together. It's a good thing to aim for, that every day there's a meal together. That's one of the benefits of having a kitchen … What is the 'high life'? Accumulating all your wealth and being on a rooftop garden by yourself? Or is it being

Figure 38 God shave the Queen (Charlton, 2018)
Source: Photo by the author.

together? There's not this kind of ... *ownership*. People just start sharing stuff in squats, which is cool. And then when you start hanging around with 'normal' people, they seem a lot more *cagey*.

Having pulled the event together and 'cracked' the space, there was definitely a sense that the organising crew had some authority. For example, halfway through the exhibition weekend, they had to make an unpopular decision to shut the roof and that incredible view:

The rooftop was obviously awesome. We had to lock that off when it got later because people were just hanging out and being noisy and getting rowdy. It's weird when you've got this 'free' space. But you have to control it to some extent, because otherwise the event is going to go ...

As well as the crew attempting to control some aspects of the event, there were also micro-negotiations over space happening all over the building. The biggest room had been claimed early on for the bands and cabaret stage, while in the former boardroom, there was a collective busy pasting anti-Royalist artwork on the walls. There was also an expensive-looking oil painting in the boardroom, which one of the squatters argued should also be protected (locked away):

Figure 39 'It's really weird that people were intimidated by this portrait' (Charlton, 2018)

Source: Photo by the author.

For some reason, which is weird, they felt that this portrait was impor- tant and we shouldn't touch it ... I think [what they did] was great to be honest. Because that's the whole point! The whole point of that board- room is it's meant to be intimidating. So, I think it's great that they flipped the power and said: 'Fuck this'. I think it's great they said 'Fuck off' to the person trying to protect it.

Throughout the building, there was no system or allocation as to which spaces people could use to display their artwork, and there was no formal selection process as to who could or could not participate. The idea behind TAA is that there is no curation – 'it is literally first come first served'. No-one controls what is considered acceptable art, the point is to open an empty building as a blank canvas for creativity and experimentation. Quinn's favour- ite night each year was the performances on the Friday, because there was 'stuff you wouldn't see any other places':

Figure 40   'It's cool that you can just come and do it and you don't have to ask anyone. You just put it up ...' (Charlton, 2018)

Source: Photo by the author.

A cabaret format. You got someone pulling out union jack bunting from her vagina. I don't know who these people are, but they're in gimp masks or some shit ... It's cool to have entertainment you wouldn't see in pubs, or most legal spaces ... It's like punk was all about saying 'fuck you' or whatever, and this is just different ways of saying fuck you through film, or music, or performances. TAA gives a great space for that to happen, because you can do whatever the fuck you want ...

The organisers and artists at TAA treasured the spontaneity, flexibility, and freedom from ownership (such as fees or curation) that the squatted space provided. But Quinn was also keen to emphasise that 'no limits' is *not* the same as 'anything goes':

You can literally do anything as long as it's not oppressive. You couldn't do like, blackface, or something that was oppressive to marginalised groups. That is not acceptable. You're creating this free space, but it's not actually free because, although it's non-curated, you are to some extent controlling it as much as you can in a way. Controlling it autonomously,

Figure 41   Love the bartender, hate the cops (Charlton, 2018)
Source: Photo by the author.

which is a complete contradiction in terms. But you've got the people [crew] who spend months thinking about it, and trying to put things in place for it, they have a vision to some extent ... Complete autonomy is impossible I think.

Something that was particularly frowned upon at TAA was 'tagging', that is, spray-painting a name or symbol over an artwork and effectively defacing someone else's work. When I asked her about it, Quinn rolled her eyes:

The number of people who just 'tag' things! Like there was a party in the wood here the other week, and people tagged the trees! But this does actually have political meaning to it, beyond scribbling on the wall. I'm not against tagging. But it's annoying when someone has spent 10 hours making a mural and the someone scribbles over it or something. Just people that ... I think on *private* property, I don't give a fuck. But when it's an autonomous space, it's good to consider other people.

At TAA 2018, property relations spilled out into the street when someone decided to tag a car which had been parked on the road outside. As it turned out, the vehicle belonged to the pub landlord next door, who soon rang the police. When the police arrived, they told some of the people on the gate that they had the possession orders to evict them and seize the

Figure 42   A bird's eye view (Charlton, 2018)
Source: Photo by the author.

sound equipment. Some people argued they were 'bullshitting you with technicalities', but others felt some responsibility towards people who had expensive equipment on the premises, and decided to shut down the music early:

> On the Saturday night, when the police came to close it down, there was loads of people disappointed that they don't get their 'Saturday night'... But other people have put thousands of pounds worth of equipment in. And I think that they *do* have hierarchy over who decides whether it carries on or not. People are like 'Oh but I want to dance!' or 'But my band hasn't played!' All of squatting is based on technicalities within the law. It's all a grey area. But so many sound systems have been taken ... Do you really want more equipment gone? ... It's easy to be rowdy when you haven't got anything [to lose] in the building.

After the squatters convinced the police that they were not holding a rave, and that they would be gone by the end of the weekend, they were left alone. The landlord, however, was frustrated and came over with a gang to 'sort out' the squatters themselves. Mace found himself on the frontline:

Yeah, the pub landlord came over with some of his mates and we had a fight. We had to fight them off at the gate. We didn't really have the personnel to fight them off. I basically had to get up there and go at these fatties like (laughs). My nose is all crunchy in different bits, but I mean we *did* fight them off.

After the fight, Quinn told me, there were some arguments around whether this was an appropriate location for TAA, and some people began to leave after threats from the landlord that they might return:

People were like 'Oh, we shouldn't have gone to a working-class area.' But it's like ... the people in the pub ... they did actual fascist threats against us. They mentioned the Football Alliance. And it's like 'Fuck them, I don't give a fuck'. On the Sunday, they were like 'There's 5000 people I can get down here now!' They mentioned there was a Tommy Robinson march on. And at the point, I thought, 'Well, I genuinely don't give a fuck your car got tagged ... let's go do it again.'

4

Making Room for Art,
the Art of Making Room

Is creativity and imagination a legitimate use of city space? If so, who gets to be creative, and who decides which activities are permissible or where they can 'appropriately' take place? Some art and artists are allocated central locations and ample room in the city, with galleries, museums, and theatres. Commissioned sculptures, or monuments judged to be 'important' and 'significant', are afforded prominent positions in public squares. Yet it's often unclear how a decision or a taste-judgement has been made, and who has claimed the authority to approve such installations. As recent direct actions against statues of colonial capitalists demonstrated – including the moment Black Lives Matter UK dragged a statue of slave trader Edward Colston off its pedestal and dumped him into the sea – there is a lack of public accountability around such decisions. But, as is also illustrated by recent criminal laws targeting those who damage public monuments, the state is heavily invested in asserting its 'ownership' of public spaces and deciding what or who is publicly significant and should be put on display. Similarly, while some highly profitable cultural activities are granted extensive space in the city, including stadiums, hotels, pubs, restaurants, and shopping centres, even 'public' parks can be temporarily enclosed to put on festivals and large concerts, forcing people to pay an extortionate sum for tickets and moving along people using the space already (such as rough sleepers). A 'licensed' concert is permitted to create soundwaves that vibrate across the city long into the night; an 'illegitimate' rave is framed as a public nuisance and borderline criminal. But even some 'permitted' events, such as the Notting Hill Carnival, with its legendary sound systems and history of resistance against white domination of public space, is framed through a racist lens as needing a heavy state (police) presence.

In contrast to a city which recognises the legitimacy of some creative spaces and not others, squats are important because they can facilitate access to and participation in art and culture. They can provide free spaces for exhibitions and performances, but also studio space, rehearsal and recording space, art and photography studios, as well as research and writing space. Squats are also important for art and culture because, insofar as staying in a squat means an escape from the wage–rent vortex, artists can free up *time* in which they can be 'unprofitable'. Particularly early on, squats are somewhere free to live to practise skills and develop talent, which is often something only accessible to those from wealthy backgrounds who have more freedom to spend their time 'unproductively' and not worry about finding somewhere to live or food to eat. Squats can provide spaces to share experimental or provocative art without having to navigate the cultural limits of established tastes in a profit-driven art scene of galleries and music venues.

Through art and culture, squats also provide spaces for collectivity and an ethic of care. To take one example, in the rave scene, some crews have named themselves 'tribes' since the late 1980s, in a kind of 'neo-tribalism'[1] which can be 'distinguished by shared lifestyles, values and understandings of what is appropriate behaviour'.[2] In their study of rural raves and drum and bass club culture, Riley, Morey and Griffin also found that community was 'reinforced by a discourse that constituted a group value ... participants described a sense of duty of care that applied to themselves, their friends and fellow partiers, and to the environment (an example being picking up litter at the end of the party)'.[3] The repetitive feel and basslines in the music are experienced not just through the ears but also through vibrations in the centre of the body which hit everybody, together, at the same time. As for dancing, it's as if 'the distinction between one and all disappears ... it is a dance to lose the self ... we dance therefore we are'.[4] Even the drugs chosen by most ravers – NOS, marijuana, MDMA (ecstasy), and liquid acid (LSD) – are meant to produce trips which create an overwhelming sense of empathy, unity, and oneness.

Yet though festivals and raves are 'an essential part of the squatting movement', they 'are seldom written about and sometimes disparaged by the political wing ... a split between *politicos* and hedonists is traditional'.[5] Because all art has the potential to *affect*, it can be the source material for belonging, solidarity, and tools for political expression. In *Stage Invasion*, poet and activist Pete the Temp Bearder argues that art is like a political toolbox. Through poetry, for example, the voice becomes 'cultural equipment for progressive change ... through our voice we represent ourselves and our communities'.[6] For Pete the Temp, art is politically significant because it has the ability to 'occupy and hold space, and then galvanise the people inside it ... live performance is a petri dish of human solidarity'.[7] Crucially, however, rather than simply *informing* others of our political campaigns from the top-down; art is important because it *involves* others – culturally, politically, and even at the level of molecules, hormones, and emotions.

We need to consider this 'chemical weaponry of affect'[8] in context. In the *Politics of Aesthetics*, Rancière argues that, ultimately, politics is not something that happens in government or even 'on the street', but instead 'revolves around what is seen and what can be said about it, around who has the ability to see and the talent to speak, around the properties of space and the possibilities of time'.[9] He therefore concludes that artistic practices are essential for politics, because they 'are "ways of doing and making" that intervene in the general distribution of ways of doing and making as well as in the relationships they maintain'. For Rancière, artworks can be radical, because they educate in a way that does not presume the inability of an audience to understand. For him, precisely because 'the meaning of artworks ... is contingent, they remain constitutively open for interpretive reconfiguration by anyone and everyone',[10] so there is a potential for the spectator of art to become emancipated.[11] A spectator is able to interpret, and be affected, by the art in ways that might go beyond the intention of the artist, and it is this contingency of art that means it has a potentially democratic and liberatory quality. Art's political promise is that it might 'allow people to see the world and their place in it differently, which may in turn lead them to intervene in it and change it by becoming political subjects, yet it can only do so *as art* by respecting their autonomy as spectators'.[12] In this way, 'an art is never just an art: it is always at the same time the proposal of a world',[13] and yet it is precisely this that 'is invariably under threat from artists and curators who aspire to "teach" their audience a particular political message'.[14]

Consequently, through experimental and boundary-crossing art, squats directly contribute to wider urban life by helping to push the limits of what we imagine to be a possible use of space. As Alan W. Moore points out, 'the wild weeds of squat culture have played an important part in some of the most significant creative movements of the late 20th and early 21st century', yet 'many states and cities are acting like gardeners who systematically cut off new growth'.[15] Instead of their creative potential being recognised, squatted spaces are either criminalised and shut down, *or* they are 'regularly recuperated by governance as part of city cultural infrastructure'.[16] In the age of 'creative city' policies, local authorities compete to invest in cultural industries, with the aim of giving 'run-down' neighbourhoods an authentic or exoticised 'edge', so that they might become ripe for investment (i.e. gentrified). Squatters can get caught up in this process insofar as they independently create 'cool' neighbourhoods in parts of the city that have high vacancy rates, which local authorities then seek to incorporate into their development of that area (usually resulting in the eviction of squatted spaces and the destruction of what made the area vibrant in the first place).

Squats provide access for those who would be denied any opportunity to express themselves through more mainstream art scenes – whether because of their background, lack of resources, or because the art they are doing doesn't fit with established tastes or is deemed too risky from a profit-making perspective. By asking who has access to art, the examples below raise a democratic question of who has access to means of expression (i.e. the resources to make oneself seen and heard). Squats provide flexible and negotiable spaces for marginalised voices and appearances. Through squats, people find a platform and a supportive community. Cultural events such as exhibitions, gigs, or raves, are an opportunity to network and come together. They facilitate community participation and belonging, providing a potential foundation for solidarity, even if they are hard to justify to those who would dismiss squats as a hedonistic or a subcultural niche. Art is a creative process that needs space and time in which to innovate and to push cultural boundaries. But in a world where only the wealthy, or those willing to take on massive amount of debt, can find the time and space to be 'unproductive', culture risks becoming stagnant, monotone, restrictive. Because they don't have to justify their use under the ownership model, squats have the potential to open up new artistic, affective, and political horizons.

PARTY POLITICS

Growing up in London, Jilly had been going to squat parties and raves from an early age, but it wasn't until her late teens that she decided to try to live in squats hoping to free up time to do art:

> It was like: 'take a space, spend some time making work, put on a show'. And then it became more of like a living thing. So, people kind of had various squats around London ... so when I was in London back from uni, I'd stay with them.

After finishing university, Jilly moved back to London and squatted in an ex-photography factory in Waterloo. There were ten bedrooms and a workshop, and the squatters also intended to use the space as a gallery, but it ended up taking on a range of different uses – meeting rooms, function rooms, a cinema, and a bar. So they could hold onto the space, the artists' collective made an agreement with the landlord to stay, so long as they would leave when asked:

> And we were there for like ... we had that for about three years or something. And when he asked us to leave ... we did, but then ... we said to him, when we were leaving: 'You know, if you leave this building unprotected it's just going to be squatted again ...' [Then] *somehow* (laughs), about two weeks after we moved out ... And he was just an idiot because he had quite an easy relationship with us and then he ended up in a much more difficult situation.

Negotiation had given the squatters extended use of the factory as somewhere to free up time and space to be creative, but when they were evicted and the landlord kept the building empty, they moved back in. The agreement was that they could use the space while it was disused, but they saw the owner as not staying true to that compromise.

Jilly squatted both because she 'needed somewhere to live', which she considered to be a material need, but simultaneously because she needed time and somewhere to belong as well:

> I have particular feelings about what I wanted to do with my *time*, not wanting to spend all my time working to pay rent, and wanting to have a space to do the work that I thought was important *politically*, and also to have spaces *with my friends* and the people that I wanted to be with. Yeah ... I guess squatting provided those things ... the *physical space*. And then also the kind of *emotional* or *mental* space to kind of think outside of the normal structures of capitalist existence or whatever. To think beyond like 'Okay, how am I going to pay my rent? How am I going to make enough money to buy food?' and all these kind of things.

Here, her personal need for space overlapped with aspirations to free up time for politics, art, community, as well as the ability to stay located in the city she was from and a part of:

> 'Things that I think are, sort of quite basic desires, like to be around people that you love and to have the time and space to do the things that you want to do... they shouldn't be extreme demands! But they are very difficult to achieve in London unless you are extremely wealthy... You

know, in London, it's like even if you just want to live with your friends...
even that is too much to ask. Let alone living with your friends and having
space in which you could *create* things and all of that not costing the earth.'

In Jilly's experience, the pressures on space and time in London were particularly extreme, and therefore it was 'harder to have the kind of life that you
want, or to do the things that you want to do, without completely changing
how you live'. She drew a direct connection between being able to access
physical spaces and having the 'mental space' to participate in creative or
political ends.

Jilly had been involved in SQUASH (Squatters Action for Secure Homes)
which had fought against both the Criminal Justice bill 1994 and then the
Legal Aid, Sentencing, and Punishment of Offenders bill in 2011/12, both
of which had sought to criminalise squatting outright. Coming from squats
which emphasised the crossovers between art, activism, and subculture,
Jilly was wary of the image of squatters which might be put out into the
media and was concerned that they might play into stereotypes which del-
egitimised their use of space. SQUASH therefore made an explicit effort to
downplay the use of space for art and culture, in order to emphasise shelter
and housing:

> We focused on criminalisation of vulnerable homeless people. And less
> on the kind of *positive* narratives. I mean ... we used Grow Heathrow
> a lot as an example and you know, the story of Grow Heathrow is not
> 'You're criminalising vulnerable homeless people', it's 'Here's a really
> positive social project that is happening with the collaboration of the local
> community and is exciting and inspiring' and so on. So, we *were* putting
> forward that positive narrative as well ... [but] what we sort of attempted
> to present was like 'ordinary people also squat as well'. I did a fair amount
> of news stuff and I would take out all my jewellery and I would do my
> hair like a normal person and present myself as far as possible as though I
> might be working for an NGO or something.

As spaces where fringe styles, alternative aesthetics, and marginalised
expressions can exist, the risk is that squats become pigeon-holed and
struggle to engage with a wider public. 'It's really important to the survival
of squatting, in my view, that it doesn't allow itself just to be completely
othered', Jilly argued:

Because when that happens, it's very easy for the rest of society to just be like 'Well, then we'll just cut off that limb', you know? I think it's important to make things be accessible and enable people to recognise themselves in you. You need to play on people's sympathies (laughs). And be like 'Hey, we're not that different, you and me, and you could be doing this too.'

Framing squatters as 'punks and hippies' is reductive and serves the purpose of making squats seem as if they are facetious, hedonistic, and apolitical places, which can be stigmatised and dismissed. But even those squats which appear, on the surface, to be shallow spaces of enjoyment, fulfil a purpose in creating social bonds:

You can have a hedonistic time and then you can go and *do stuff!* (laughs) I think that, for me personally, having really great parties is really important. It enables and sustains and revitalises the work that you need to do … you're creating space for connections and enjoyment and fun which is outside of the capitalist structures.

Anti-capitalist politics here takes the form of creating 'free' spaces, where there are no economic limitations to organising a gathering or which places a limit on who may or may not (in principle) participate. For Jilly, this played into her anarchist principles, but she was quick to add that some squatters had a different idea of anarchism, which she considered to be more libertarian and individualistic:

For some people, anarchism means nobody ever tells me what to do. I'm not bound by anything. I'm not bound by the people around me. I'm not bound by my community. I'm never going to commit to anything beyond this moment. And I'm just going to do exactly what my instinct is telling me to do right now. And that might be to stay in bed all day, or it might be to, you know, whatever … And then [for] other people, well I guess certainly for me, there's freedom *and* autonomy. [Anarchism] requires the ability to formulate intentions that you can then work towards and to be able to control your own urges, in order that you can achieve things that you want to do and to be able to do that collectively as well. To be able to say: 'We as a collective want to achieve this thing.'

Jilly wasn't completely dismissive of such individualism, but she argued that it failed to recognise the potential for cultural spaces to provide a very practical and material purpose of keeping cross-city networks together, maintaining a sense of belonging and collective empowerment, and supporting collective action:

> You know, you certainly get lots of squats where people are very individualised and where everybody basically just looks out for themselves ... [they] aren't trying to create a collective because they feel that their freedom and autonomy lies in just doing exactly what *they* want at all times.

While pointing out that there are different 'types' of squatting, Jilly's experience in cultural and artistic squats was that creative spaces provided something of the lifeblood of squatting in London. By creating connections, identity, and affect, these spaces are valuable nodes of the network which can bring people together and potentially strengthen ties across the city:

> I think having spaces is essential to building *power*. And, you know, just having physical spaces in which people can come together, share ideas, build relationships, and which are outside of capitalist control, is really *really* important. And the fact is that that's, you know, extremely difficult ... impossible ... to achieve in London in other ways.

Squatters are stigmatised for being part of a hedonistic subculture. Yet, on the other hand, by providing free spaces for enjoyment and cultural participation, this side of squatting also provides an opportunity for solidarity, community, and even inclusion of wider publics. As Jilly put it, the everyday 'process and activity of squatting is time-consuming, tiring, and has a tendency to become quite self-obsessive ... and lose sight of the issues that are affecting everyone else'. But in these spaces, there is also potential to engage with issues related to or beyond maintaining and opening squats. Counter-intuitively, while cultural and artistic spaces were perhaps the strongest expression of squatting as subcultural, they were also the spaces where squatters might 'break out' of an activist ghetto by expressing urban issues beyond squatting and creating new solidarities in response. If you have squatted space, it provides people who want to express things considered unacceptable by mainstream culture and discourse, the opportunity to have some power over what they can say and do.

BACKSTAGE AT THE RAVE

Figure 43   Patchwerk Sound System (Hackney Marshes, 2019)
Source: Photo by a participant.

Gids lives in a sparsely furnished council flat in Brentford. There's a sofa, an enormous sound system, some traffic signs, as well as a street-cleaning trolley which he has redesigned to conceal a portable record deck and mixer. He doesn't sit down at any point during our interview and paces around the flat. At each pause in the conversation, he beatboxes or makes sounds like a Jungle MC. 'Right, I'm going to stay on my feet and make more tea and coffee, do you want another one?' From the kitchen next door, he continues to tell me about his involvement in both squats and London's rave scene after leaving the army:

> I'd come out of the regular forces. So, you don't even know about sign-ing-on when you come out, never mind some fucking squatting kind of thing, you know? So, I went to Advisory Service for Squatters ... straightaway it was *political*. So that got me interested, I suppose, because [squatting] is looking at inequality ... it's rebelliousness. It was disobedi-ent. It wasn't doing as I was told, but it was *right* as far as I felt.

Figure 44 'This guy did the best set I heard all night. He played at 9 p.m. on Sunday. Did a live Acid-Techno set on a fucking Roland 808 drum machine and a little synthesiser keyboard and his laptop. He smashed it.' (Hackney Marshes, 2019)

Source: Photo by a participant.

Being involved in squats, Gids soon developed an interest in all things dance music and went to his first 'great big warehouse party' in the East End around 1988/9:

> It was like a Jamaican sound system. They'd gone into this building there. And for me, that was like, one of the greatest things ever. It was like, wow, that's the drugs, you can *feel* this. White working-class guy ... *I didn't know you could like yourself that much*, do you know what I mean?'

As well as simply enjoying going to raves, there was a clear ethic behind Gids' view of free parties, which tied in with his politics and his post-military job as a youth worker:

> I'd just started a community youth work two-year course at Goldsmiths and part of the course is training yourself, going into areas that you've never done before ... I picked All Saints Road, where there was the Mangrove Community Association, black-led, where the British Black Panthers were basically founded from there.

Later, Gids got involved with the squatted Cooltan Art Centre in Brixton, with the intention of bringing anti-racism and his experience working with marginalised youth into the space. His aim was to engage the local community by bringing in sound system culture, but he tells me he faced some push-back from the crew:

I was doing a set of parties, determined to get young black people in there. Jungle had just come out and I said: 'Right, we're going to do jungle.' It was at the group meeting [and] this Egyptian guy ... 'No man, can't be bringing all them blacks in here ...' No one questions him. And he's kind of like 'It shouldn't be allowed.' So, I took 'It Shouldn't Be Allowed' and that's what I called the parties (laughs). We aimed that at the Criminal Justice Act [1994] kind of thing.

Squatting aligned with Gids' politics in other ways too. 'There's definitely a political edge' to squat parties, he said:

That you take an empty building and that you open it up and that within ten minutes of it being open, the first spell is spray paint and graffiti artists are in. You're not excluding them. You're including 15 year olds ... it's non-licensed. It's done completely differently. Mostly peacefully, cooperatively, not-for-profit.

In an effort to educate people on politics and history at the raves, Gids showed me the 'splashboards' he had made, using 'For Sale' and 'Sold' signs from outside buildings to create collages about past protest movements and the squatting scene. He'd found that the best place to display this exhibition had been the chillout spaces at raves:

At 4 o clock in the morning, when they're all spinning round or whatever, and you've got herbal tea ... [we] have a shared experience, some interactivity, and then hit them with political stuff ... stick them up round the marquee. 'That's Newbury [anti-roads protest] that is ...' So, the idea is to kind of hit people with some info and, like I say, what I've found with it, I've had my stuff from here quoted back at me ... you're getting different people involved, aren't you?

While Gids certainly saw squatting as a 'necessity', then, this was a broader definition than that of most squatters. Politics and enjoyment were also nec-

Figure 45   'It's a pub called the Bitter End. We never actually squatted it; the building owner gave us permission to use it.' (Romford, 2019)

Source: Photo by a participant.

essary, and his view on squatting simply didn't fit within a hedonism vs. political binary:

> I suppose it's everything about *living* really. Anything that goes on in a house or a home, you can apply that to squatting. If you ever go to a party, a *decent* party in a community-led open space, open community, transient ... you've got your core group that hold it together ... some can manage it themselves, some can only manage it by popping [pills], taking other things and doing all sorts of stuff, you know. And that's when you notice there's a *need*. It's about caring and fucking *healing* ... Someone said recently 'Have you done any youth work recently, Gids?' And it's like, 'Fuck, it's all youth work at 60 mate!' (laughs)

I'd met Gids at the same spoken-word event at Grow Heathrow as Heddy, where he had been actively encouraging him to do more poetry and performances. It was clear that his experiences as a youth worker and the ethic of care which guided this, was something he found in a diversity of squatted spaces – whether parties, housing, community centres, or a combination.

Figure 46 'We have transformed that building ... we don't do raves there. It's shitting on your own doorstep really, isn't it?' (Romford, 2019)

Source: Photo by a participant.

Heddy was also into the rave scene and was a co-founder of Patchwerk sound system, a free party crew which – at the time – were based in a closed pub in Romford and putting on events in parks and warehouses across London. While staying at the Runnymede Eco-Village in 2015, an environmentalist and pro-democracy land squat, Heddy had met like-minded people who loved their music, were obsessed with musical equipment, and were attracted by the freedom and belonging the free party scene had to offer:

> You get a different level of freedom with these types of events than you would with any other type. Squatters are going for the level of freedom. Everybody wants to go out on the weekend! But you go to a shitty club where you're going to get searched, pay loads of money, queue, drinks are expensive, it's not well lit, you're listening to music you don't necessarily want to listen to ... As event organisers, if we try and do events in venues ... it's impossible unless you *own* a venue because there's just so many overheads.

The ethos behind Patchwerk sound system was simply to bring people together. Anyone, in principle, was welcome, and the system itself was a

Figure 47 'When I take drugs at a party, especially the outdoor ones, and I got nothing to do, litter picking is my thing. It rubs off on other people.' (Hackney Marshes, 2019)

Source: Photo by a participant.

manifestation of this inclusivity: a patchwork rig of different people bringing speakers and amplifiers, connecting it all together to build something impressive:

> We're a patchwork crew in the sense that we're all from different backgrounds, but we all do parties. So, most of us have our own speakers anyway ... big carbon fibre horns that go on top (from a cinema!). Horns are better for indoors because you have more control of where your sound is going. Then we got two Y-bins [subwoofers], which look like a 'Y' when you look from above. And we've got 4 'W' bins which are single-driver ones.

While Heddy preferred outdoor raves, there was more control over the sound in warehouses, which meant less risk of drawing unwanted attention or simply bothering people living nearby:

> At Hackney Marshes, there's only so loud you can go before you just start annoying everybody. With the flats and such around here. So, we just take a small part of the sound system for that really. If we put all the sound system together, it's a ludicrous display of speakers (laughs). We've never had the opportunity to take it all out into one space.

At a rave on Hackney Marshes in 2018, two men had started fighting over which genre of music was better, jungle or techno – 'people get aggro about silly things', Heddy sighed. When trouble happens, the Patchwerk crew 'generally turn the music off and everyone who is confident from the rig goes over, basically'. Unfortunately, as he is quite tall, this often landed on Heddy's shoulders, even if he protested that he 'didn't like fighting … I'm fucked [high] and I've got glasses! (laughs).' Luckily, however, 'a lot of the time you get protected by the fact that the party has a good vibe … the party protects itself.' Because people want the party to carry on, there is a lot of respect for the crews that put it on, as well as a desire to keep trouble and unwanted police presence to a minimum.

For this reason, Heddy preferred the outdoor raves because they brought a sense of freedom and liberty:

No physical restrictions. You got the freedom of a free party, in the sense that you can do what you want. You've also got no physical boundaries. In a warehouse, you got physical boundaries, sometimes you got a big outdoor space, but when you're outside it sounds different. You can tune your speakers a lot nicer outside. You not got to think about any type of acoustic obstructions. I mean that can be interesting as well. Sometimes when you do a building, and you've got weird pillars and stuff, you do need to take them into account in your soundchecks. It's much better to be outside in open space to make it sound good.

Finding spaces outside for a free party lent itself to creating communal moments, removing material obstructions for the sound waves and for bodies. As the pulse of the music vibrates through everyone simultaneously, it can create a sense of oneness. For Heddy, there were some substances that could heighten this experience, but there were also others that could damage the peaceful and collective aims of the party:

I don't do Ket. Ketamine is the downfall of the party scene sometimes, because you end up with Ket Zombies everywhere. I don't personally do it. NOS is one of the only ways that people make money off of raves. We vote on it as a community before we do parties: are you going to sell gas or not? I always vote no to gas. Because I'm not inclined about making money and I don't like the way it can affect the party. But then I generally do get out-voted and we have a democratic process, so … we do gas. But sometimes we don't ... When you do an outdoor party down the marshes, you've got no way of charging entry. You can go round asking for donations but it's usually unsuccessful, people think you're just a blagger. So, the only way you can really make money is by having a bar or by selling gas, so we can make a profit.

As the space is negotiated between different people, however, free parties still act as regular get-togethers that keep London's squatting network close. Those who attend emphasise collective freedom and social organisation away from the state and formal institutions. This means that organising and/or participating in the free party scene can create infrastructure – both materially and socially – for further collective projects:

Pretty much all the people involved in raves are squatters, especially in London. It's mainly organised by squatters. A lot of the speakers [equipment] lives in squats as well. It is mainly attended by squatters as well. It's the squat network that we do our promotion through in a sense. A lot of promoting is you just send a text to someone who lives in a squat, and then they tell everyone in the squat sort of thing, like an organic phone tree system, letting everybody know, It's one of the impressive things about the squat scene in London. One of the things that's engrossed me and kept me here, is that it's just so well connected. Everybody seems to know each other and even if you don't, you at least know somebody who knows that person.

What may look like people just having fun, in other words, takes on a politics in a city like London. As gatherings in public spaces are more and more heavily policed, the only options become festivals and venues with high overheads and ticket prices to match. It's the material gathering which becomes politically charged, even if there's no explicit political material or message. The ends and the means overlap, or, as Heddy put it:

Party and politics, they're so highly linked ... it's *our* party, like you've got the Tory Party, the Lib Dem Party, the Labour Party and all that, ours is the *free* party. And it doesn't fit into the same narrative as like the political parties, but free parties are a very political thing because they're how we represent ourselves ... that's our party, that's our representation. And yeah, sometimes it doesn't come across in the right way and we could do it a lot better and be less hedonistic and more like pointful, but that's our representation of our way of life ... that sparks something in people, like some either creative or activist thing within people and it shows you that we can make a stand.

THE HAMMER WITH WHICH WE SHAPE IT

Spurred on by the London 2012 Olympics, the whole of Fish Island had become a building site as developers rushed to Hackney Wick, knocking down industrial warehouses and replacing them with flats overlooking the canal. We passed heavily graffitied buildings by the station, with giant letters reading 'From Shithouse to Penthouse', before Vylet guided me away from the hipster-looking breweries and bars and took me instead to her regular greasy spoon café. We each got a cup of tea and pulled out a metal seat on each side of a row of tables. 'To be honest, I don't consider myself an artist' she took a sip before continuing:

I went to uni doing Film Studies, but I didn't learn anything. It was more theory and media studies, which was interesting, but I wanted to *make* and I wanted to *create* and I wanted to be *inspired*. I saw [squatting] as a chance into another world where things were happening, and people were doing things.

Dropping out of university at 18, Vylet found herself 'in a really rubbish job and just feeling like ... what am I doing? Where am I going?' By squatting, she argued:

You are living on a line. But that line can be life, as in actually *enjoying* ... like I never had a debt because I never had credit, because I lived out of food from skips and I found my clothes and my television and my furniture on the streets. So, I never had to buy those things ... you could live really, really, really cheaply when you lived on the line.

Directionless and looking for something to scratch the creative itch, Vylet began going to free parties and getting involved with underground sound systems, even organising her own regular gigs at a pub in Walthamstow:

I was like 'I like this! This is good!' ... I kind of sucked it all in and went and moved into a squat with some friends and it felt very *very* like this was taking me in a direction that I wanted to go in. I wanted to be a filmmaker ... to make creative things happen. I felt like this was a chance to get creative and I started painting backdrops and stuff like that.'

For Vylet, attending free parties was both a creative outlet and something to belong to, to be part of. Squatting was a way to keep dedicating time and energy to a vocation she was passionate about, rather than work a job just to meet rent.

We were really kind of *transforming* spaces. And there wasn't a commission. It was doing it because we *wanted* to do it ... you don't get that space anywhere else. These days, [space] is just astronomical. The overheads. You can't be creatively expressive just for the fun of it. Just through the *passion* of it. There isn't the space to do that.

Vylet argued that, while squatting residential buildings had become more difficult, it hadn't really changed the buildings that artists and creatives were using. Coming from a 'very arts-based road into squatting and into reclaiming space', she explained that they were already mostly using (and living in) vacant commercial properties even before the change in law:

I mean, they *were* our homes, [but] we weren't really living in residential properties anyway: we were taking empty commercial spaces. Because we wanted longevity, we weren't taking places that had been newly done up, that somebody was going to move into next week ... we would deliberately take places that were disused and unloved because we wanted to have space [and] we wanted to have *time* in those places.

Opening up spaces for sleeping, creating, and putting on events, Vylet's crew also had a unique insight of the sheer extent of vacancy across the city:

Literally, there was somewhere we partied in 1998 and then we went back and did a TAA [Temporary Autonomous Art] in 2008 ... our DJ list was like [still on the wall] (laughs). It was like nothing had changed. No one had touched it. And we were like saying to the landlord: 'You haven't used this space, let us stay here!' But ultimately, they were waiting to get the offer from developers to knock it down and turn it into [unaffordable] flats and that is what we've seen across all of those big empty spaces ... now you have these spaces that actually aren't affordable for locals, so they're still getting pushed out.

The coffee grinder kept going off, so I pushed the voice recorder closer across the table, skidding across some loose grains of sugar. Vylet began to explain the ethos that motivated her to put on events and dedicate her time to art and culture. She was someone who aspired to be an artist, a filmmaker, but had found this a difficult world to access when coming from a working-class background. Squatting was a way in:

In terms of where I come from ... I'm not estranged from my parents so, yes, I could go home and live with my parents at any time. But I didn't want to do that! (laughs) I don't want to go backwards, I want to go forward and make my own life. So, I guess in some ways I did have options, whereas other people wouldn't have had options.

Squatted spaces were more inclusive than the established art world, where you seemed to need the privilege of a wealthy background, networks, or the right 'taste', in order to find the space and time to be creative. Squats, on the other hand, make room for experimentation, pushing the boundaries of taste without financial or class boundaries to that expression:

It was that idea that bringing people into a reclaimed space, where they weren't being *charged* and they weren't being *judged* ... within the art world, there is both of those two things. You either know the 'right people' to make shit work, and you're going to get into galleries anyway, you've got the money ... [or] you have to be a 'certain standard'. You have to be playing a certain game ... I mean, you can't afford art space, it's just not there. And I think by reclaiming those spaces for ourselves we were able to make space for that kind of expression and creative output ... it's about having free access and non-commercialised access to spaces. There is this whole like 'How do we get marginalised people involved? How do we get poorer people involved? How do we get ...' and it's like, ultimately, you have to reduce the overheads to the arts.

Vylet saw squats as a space where class boundaries could even be challenged, warped, and crossed. For example, she told me about people involved in the party scene who were from backgrounds which were (relatively) wealthier compared to others, sometimes referred to as 'trustafarians':

[who] had an inheritance and they wanted a sound system and they wanted to kind of do that. So, they'd buy a big truck and they'd kind of

have this lifestyle. And I think that there's also always been the people that were born on [new age] traveller sites or like, literally with nothing other than that life. And I think there's always been that spectrum. And I think that's what's kind of quite exciting about it, is actually the fact that it cuts across so many different classes and it's really quite interesting.

Vylet had been an early organiser with TAA and was part of the crew who set up and ran the first events back in the early 2000s. TAA was a platform where emerging and marginalised artists could share their work and gain confidence in their craft:

> I think there was a lot of people that came through what we were doing with TAA, a lot of artists that we encouraged to have confidence in their work, that have now taken that somewhere. A lot of people ... just confidence in themselves and I think that there is definitely a sense that we not only achieved something, but we also pulled ourselves up and what we can achieve.

TAA created a space to meet people who were part of the wider 'squatter' community, but who were perhaps geographically dispersed, as well as being a space to get to know people that wanted to come and join in:

> We had people coming [into squats] all the time. It was always evolving ... [TAA] would be a way to kind of meet people. And we had a lot of people who were living on the streets that came and took part in that and then became part of the crew and ended up living with us and moving around with us. So, it was definitely not just like: we're *us* and that's it. And I think that that was what was also beautiful is that people would find their way. The synergy of kind of being somewhere and meeting people and it was quite fluid because we would open our doors.

For her, these spaces were something to be celebrated, although she also recognised their challenges and limitations. Through her long involvement in TAA, squat parties, and squats, however, Vylet also had vast experience of some of the problems and limitations that could arise. I got us a refill of tea before she continued:

> I also agree that a lot of these events that happen within squats are very self-centred and happen within a bubble. And that was always my

argument for wanting to take [TAA] *out of squats* and where I am now is because, ultimately, I got really tired of preaching to the converted ... [but] as soon as you took it out of the squat, it changed the parameters.

Organising an event in a squat is simultaneously a way to open the doors for participation, offering up walls for exhibition space as well as rooms for stages or platforms for speaking and being heard, but it also risked putting up new barriers. In wanting to be inclusive and democratic, TAA welcomed anyone to take part in the organisation of the event, but Vylet argued this only led to more perspectives, disagreements, and indecision:

I think we could have gone a lot further and done a lot more had we not had to have more of a horizontal functioning. However, I'm not an anarchist, because I don't actually believe that that works ... there was always a few of us who was doing everything and then a layer of people who would sometimes get involved and then a layer of people that always wanted to have their voice heard, but never actually did anything. And I think that I would definitely say, from my experience, that there was a few of us who had the vision as well. Not everyone can have the vision.

The fact that there were a few people who were 'doing everything' reflects both an unequal distribution of labour, but also an internal hierarchy in which some were (potentially) able to claim more authority over the space than others. Again, while not based on any notion of 'ownership' and more open to the possibility of negotiation, this doesn't mean property relations within the space were always accountable:

When the sound system crew saw that actually we [TAA] were like achieving something that was sustainable they were like: 'Oh maybe we're going to start taking you seriously.' (laughs) It was quite interesting that my voice as a woman started to get listened to ... I think what was really amazing was actually interestingly the squat party scene where we came from, very male-dominated. And you had to have the loudest voice and it was definitely very alpha in terms of who got listened to. And I think that when we started kind of doing our own thing ... it was female-led and I think that's always been a really good thing about it. The women were generally calling the shots a lot more ... there were men involved, obviously. But I think that that made it quite different.

The aim to have inclusive organisational structures may have made it difficult to make decisions and get stuff done, but it also meant that there were opportunities for people to take the helm and steer who might usually not be given that recognition. Artistic and creative expression within these spaces offered new opportunities to be heard and seen. As a mode of expression, a way to communicate feeling, and to affect others, someone who wasn't being listened to could potentially find a way to get a point across.

For Vylet, this is why art has liberatory potential. As someone who suggested that she would not be putting on events or doing art *at all* if it wasn't for squatting, she argued that finding space and time for creative work was also finding space and time for social change. We'd got to the bottom of our mugs and the conversation seemed to be drawing to a close, but she ended our conversation with a quote from Brecht:

'Art shouldn't be a mirror to society, it should be the hammer with which we shape it.' Art has that role. And right from the very beginning of what [TAA] were doing was that idea that taking art out of the sterile environment where it's quite elitist and people don't feel that they have access to it. Ultimately, when you take the *access* to art away from people, you take away that *ability to communicate* art. Not only communicate what's good; it communicates what's bad, it communicates hopes and fears, and it can *galvanise*. When you look throughout history, art has always played ... art and culture always play an important part in any movement of people, any movement of the society ... ultimately, *that is how we shift society* and how we communicate. Opening access to the arts to people who don't have access to it is really key. And I think that's where art within squats can play that role ... people who are on the streets maybe actually need that more than others.

TEMPORARY. AUTONOMOUS. ART.

The three words that make up TAA – temporary, autonomous, art – help us to understand the stakes of squatting. 'Temporariness' is reflective of precarity, but it also means freedom from the bureaucracy, formality, and challenge of maintaining a permanent space in a city dominated by the ownership model. 'Autonomy' means living by your own rules – 'auto' and 'nomos' – but can play out very differently from squat to squat, particularly in terms of actions which disrupt one another's use or safety in a space. And finally, 'art', the possibility of expression, voice, appearance, affect, a platform and a space from which to be seen and heard, and all the possibilities and politics associated with this.

Using the website Squat Radar to contact squats in different cities, Quinn had hitchhiked around Europe without any money, but performing music in exchange for somewhere to stay. One of the spaces that stuck in her memory was a five-storey building in Bilbao which had been squatted for twelve years and included a free restaurant, climbing wall, creche, and studios dedicated to screen-printing and music:

> It was like in the heart of a community, and everyone was organising this protest to … like nobody wanted this place to be evicted, the whole community was there. There were grandparents with their grandchildren, and it was just amazing to see that I could be like the heart of a community, in a way, and everything was free or you know … pay-what-you-want.

Quinn also visited the infamous Metelkova, a squatted military base in Slovenia's capital, Ljubljana. Here she was inspired by the amazing street art and sculptures, the infoshop, as well as the gig venues which operated without an entrance fee and where people could bring their own drinks.

Returning home, she wanted to set something up in her own city. The first vacant building they squatted had already been stripped of all wiring and copper, resulting in no electricity, and yet they ended up living in that space for 'five years, maybe even longer'. Outside of London, the police and landlords seemed unfamiliar with the law, and often tried to evict them by force. 'You just get used to that conflict,' Quinn sighed, 'The conflict is part of the squatting, and actually, the sooner you have the conflict, the more reassuring in a way! When you don't hear anything, it's more scary!' In one incident, when a landlord had tried to outsmart the squatters by breaking into a different part of the building, the police turned up and warned the landlord that he couldn't evict them by force, 'and I think that was the point where we were like wow, the squatting law does actually work!'

In the end, however, their longevity actually came through a successful negotiation with the landlord, promising they would look after the building on his behalf:

> So we had a conversation with him. We chose basically the cutest one, which was me (laughs), and the scariest one, which was this guy who's like a seasoned 'new age traveller' I guess. So, he was the hardest one and I was the most innocent-looking one. And the landlord actually was like 'Oh,

that's not what I expected squatters to be like, I thought all squatters were heroin addicts. Do you guys want to look after the place for me?'

For the first few months, they successfully organised a series of events designed for engaging with 'the public', including free language lessons, as well as a free people's kitchen and gigs. Yet, despite their attempts to open the space up, they still faced the prejudices of the public: 'people definitely shouted, you know, scumbags and freeloaders and stuff like that at us!' The centre also had its fair share of internal difficulties. Quinn told me about 'passive aggressive males' who 'just couldn't talk about their emotions and were always making digs at each other'. She had an in-joke with some of the others in the squat that whenever a woman said something, she would be ignored, before a guy would then repeat the same thing and everyone would pay attention to him. Setting up the squat in autumn, the crew also had to decide whether they were going to shelter homeless people knocking on the door asking if they could come in from the cold:

> And yeah, we hadn't really agreed what we'd do in that situation. And there was a couple and we let them in, then in the middle of the night they were having massive arguments and like started throwing stuff at each other ... we let them stay the night but then the next day we were like okay, you guys have to go now ... It's a difficult one because the immediate effect is someone doesn't have a roof over their head and they need a roof over their head ... [but] the other effect is that like in that situation ... then you have to put the time in to care for them, otherwise they probably are going to destroy the space.

Yet while the occupation threw up all sorts of contradictions and challenges in practice, Quinn was keen to emphasise the sense of autonomy that they found, which was an ethos that eventually attracted her to join TAA. 'We were allowed to imagine this completely different world where all the structures that we've been brought up with don't exist', she said:

> There's definitely an escapism and also, like with the TAA last week, it was like we kind of created a small utopia for a couple of days and then we were *reminded of the reality that we lived in* as, like, psycho landlords smashed glasses in our face. So, it's like we live in a very violent system ... even if we can just exist for a few days together and feel free to do that ...

Quinn did not have any desires to push for a more formal or non-squatted version of TAA, yet she recognised and knew first-hand the difficulty of putting on these events:

> You're playing with laws, you're treading on this grey area. It's obviously not legal to put on an unlicensed event. And even squatting is quite easy to get you out quite quickly if they can prove that you're going to do something illegal there.

The temporariness of squatted space allows for some freedom. To make a space anything more than temporary, in the context of the ownership model of property, would mean someone having to be recognised as the legal 'owner' and making them solely accountable for the space. It would also mean having to *justify* the space and what happens within it, including meeting bureaucratic demands and making the project financially viable:

> This country is just getting more and more bureaucratic and, like, even small community events and festivals and stuff like that is, like, more and more difficult to do then because to be able to put on a festival in your local park, you have to, like, know how to fill out a form that's full of, like, complicated questions ... squatting, in a way, is a way that we can instantly do something. Like with the TAA [in Charlton], we were evicted from the first building within three days. And everyone just came together and opened another building.

Temporariness is difficult when you get evicted at short notice and struggle to protect the space against the power and authority of the ownership model of property. Yet it is also an opportunity to find space away from that model and skate around its limits:

> At the moment it does provide lots of different possibilities. Even though it is a marginalised thing, there's lots of different types of groups using it to do different things. Whereas, yeah, whether it's having conversations, raising funds, raising awareness, symbolic actions, direct housing and, yeah, it's kind of scary because the Tories do just want to take away any possibility of anything different or any way of us not having to work full-time in order to pay mortgages which we're then in debt to for the rest of our lives.

'I guess it's about pushing the limits of what you can do in a space, what's possible', Quinn argued, 'You don't have to ask anyone's permission. I guess that relates to autonomy as well in a way, like creating these temporary spaces where anything we want to happen can happen.' However, what *autonomy* means can be very different in different spaces. What it *means* to live by your own rules, and what that looks like in practice, can vary from building to building, crew to crew, city to city, as the context that they are defining themselves against can shift, or be framed in different ways. Living by your own rules can also lead to an overemphasis of how separated, or 'outside', a crew think they are from the norms and structures of wider society:

> I think it's lovely to think that we can create like truly autonomous spaces. Like I think that having the ... I think what anarchism allows you to do that maybe ... I don't know, the reason I like anarchism more than any other political belief is because we are allowed to imagine this completely different world where all the structures that we've been brought up with don't exist ... *But then we've been influenced by this our whole lives*, like, I don't know ... if we don't recognise those privileges we're in complete denial and like everything we're doing is pointless in a way.

Quinn had a few illustrations of social structures which can persist in ostensibly inclusive and autonomous spaces:

> If you are a migrant, then do you have like an unsafe asylum case or whatever, then you can't really risk being in that situation ... Like you have to be in a safe place I guess, it's not safe ... there's a lot of reasons why people wouldn't want to enter that space. Including like mothers with children as well. And also, the squats are usually not inclusive to people in wheelchairs ... like in the TAA building, there was a lift, but we couldn't get it working. We had electricians as well and they couldn't get it working.

She also had a particularly harrowing example from the first squat she had set up in her home city. One of her friends had been sexually assaulted at the squat, but, in her words, 'people didn't want to deal with it'. Suffering from mental illness, her friend had struggled to make her voice heard within the space or to confront the person directly, so they tried to set up an 'accountability process', but 'the guy denied it and wasn't interested in participating in such a thing'. Dealing with resurfaced trauma from the attack, her friend decided to take her own life.

As an 'autonomous' space, the question of accountability is hard to navigate: seeing the space as an island or bubble can lead to a denial of the persistence of, for example, structures of gendered violence and domestic relations from the society 'outside'. There is also a hesitancy to bring in the state or criminal justice system:

> I guess the main thing is, is if you're going to hate the police, if you're going to spray ACAB [all cops are bastards] everywhere, that when these things happen we have to be ready to deal with them within our communities. And that is going to be uncomfortable. But if we don't deal with them at all, that's worse than calling the police and using the law I think.

Because they are not part of wider judicial system, there are possibilities for more imminent, extra-judicial and *restorative* justice, rather than deferring to the formal judicial system and pushing these issues away from the community. Yet this approach also relies on a crew that are willing to reflect on the ways they are *not* autonomous and still part of the structures and hierarchies of wider society, so they can be made accountable for their actions. Quinn was particularly aware of her own position and how it played out within squatted spaces. Rather than seeing her autonomy as dependent upon finding spaces where she could be *removed* from wider social structures, she saw it as crucial to address the exclusions and inequalities which persisted in squatted spaces directly, which might then allow them to live in a different way:

> I think people in the UK are not direct enough with each other. And if we could learn to maybe just be like it's okay to talk about issues and it doesn't mean I don't like you as a person, it just means that I'm not happy with this action that you did … I've heard in Brighton that people have successfully done it like in the activist scene where someone's been accused of something and they admit that they've done it and then they kind of both have support groups and then they can work together to find a solution.

As a musician, Quinn was keen to emphasise that putting on unlicensed artistic and cultural events meant they could 'play' with the limits and boundaries of how space 'should or should not' be used. For instance, while she wasn't a massive fan of tagging (especially after what had happened in Charlton), Quinn also recognised that this was an example of finding freedom away from the cultural limits of taste and 'what counts' as art or 'who counts' as an artist:

> I always thought that tagging and stuff is like a working-class art in a way, like people compare you know like the street art painting here, which is legitimised and gets funding from the Arts Council sometimes. Like people legitimise that but then maybe the kind of letter-style people don't respect it as much, even though like given the same amount of time like I think there's just as much skill in it, *it's just what people choose to do.*

Similarly to others, Quinn also recognised the financial limitations of operating within the ownership model. She celebrated the fact that squats allowed people to put on events without overheads, but also emphasised the closed economy that these spaces could maintain which can help to put on future events:

> I think that's why squatting is great, especially in London and places that it's hard to put gigs on. Because you're not paying a hire fee, you keep all the bar profits and you can do it as a benefit gig. Or if you want to have a mad line-up with people from all over the place you can do that.

The 'art' of TAA is made possible by the 'temporariness' and (relative) 'autonomy' of the space. For Quinn, squatting means spaces in which people could live and act in an alternative way, and connect with each other outside of the limits of space and time asserted by the ownership model and ideas of what or who counts as legitimate uses or users of the city:

> Squatting can allow you to live life in a different way and have more time for relationships and eating together and, you know, simple things like that. And yeah, it's nice to be able to see some beauty in life while the whole system's just like collapsing (laughs).

OLD IDEAS NEED NEW BUILDINGS

In *The Death and Life of Great American Cities*, her rallying cry against the uniformity of top-down 'meat cleaver' approaches to city space, which were bluntly destroying urban life through planning and development, Jane Jacobs argued that 'cities need old buildings so badly it is probably impossible for vigorous streets and districts to grow without them'.[17] Speaking of empty buildings as if they were ingredients for cooking up urban life, she pointed out that:

> If a city area has only new buildings, the enterprises that can exist there are automatically limited to those that can support the high costs of new construction ... these high costs of occupying new buildings may be levied in the form of rent, or they may be levied in the form of an owner's interest and amortisation payments on the capital costs of construction ... for this reason, enterprises that support the cost of new construction must be capable of paying a relatively high overhead to that necessarily required by old buildings. To support such high overheads, the enterprise must either (a) high profit or (b) well subsidized ... only operations that are well established, high-turnover, standardised or heavily subsidized can afford, commonly, to carry the costs of new construction ...[18]

Among the examples Jacobs gives, she observes that 'well-subsidized opera and art museums often go into new buildings', and yet 'the unformalized feeders of the arts – studios, galleries, stores for musical instruments and art supplies, backrooms where the low earning power of a seat and a table can absorb uneconomic discussions – these go into old buildings'.[19] New buildings tended to support existing and low-risk ideas which had a proven track-record in high profits or attracting subsidies, but old buildings did not carry such overheads and limits to what could be imagined and created therein. She concludes:

> For really new ideas of any kind – no matter how ultimately profitable or otherwise successful some of them might prove to be – there is no leeway for such chancy trial, error and experimentation in the high-overhead economy of new construction. Old ideas can sometimes use new buildings, New ideas must use old buildings.[20]

Though tending to couch this argument in the language of the market – including the potential for profitability and 'enterprise' – Jacobs' logic is nevertheless useful in considering the art, culture, and politics supported by squats.

Squats make direct use of old buildings, providing studios, storage, venues, that make room for art and culture. By providing somewhere to live outside of the wage–rent vortex, they also allow time to be dedicated to being 'unprofitable'. Squats allow artists to circumnavigate established tastes, which are themselves expressed *spatially*, by being granted recognised gallery, theatre, and concert space, or prominent positions in public spaces. In contrast, squats can be incredibly creative and experimental, simultaneously pushing the boundaries of property ownership and imagination. Not all art has to be successful in expanding new horizons. But it's in the trial and error, the development of skills, and the ability to allocate energy to experimentation as part of a creative community, that this becomes a possibility. The problem is, capitalist culture feeds off such innovation, creativity, and diversity, and those subcultures that can't be subsumed into profitable investments or creative city (gentrification) policies often find themselves evicted. Charles Landry[21] is surely correct to say that 'city-making is an art, not a formula ... the skills required to re-enchant the city are far wider than the conventional ones like architecture, engineering and land-use planning'. Yet the question remains: *where* are the spaces in which these skills can exist? Who is able to access them, and how creative and aspirational they are able to be?

In the Netherlands, for instance, the Dutch 'Broadplaatsen' (breeding places) programme saw disused spaces being made available to artists and cultural industries, in a way that saw 'the squatters' do-it-yourself logic re-articulated in the language of the creative industry. In this context, squatters do not represent a threat, but rather an asset to the political economy.'[22] As Vincent Boschma observes, in Amsterdam, 'policymakers realised the important part that these places have played in the cultural and creative life of Amsterdam generally and in launching the careers of emerging artists in particular,'[23] and sought to allocate city funds for working with groups of artists that wanted to set up projects in the city. However, through this programme, they also sought to control squatting and artists, demanding a subsidised rent (which many could not afford) meaning that:

> most spaces go to young and hip graphic design and digital media companies or agencies focused on commercial, market-driven products and popular media ... hardly anything experimental or interesting is taking place in breeding-places ... the focus tends to be on affirmations of mainstream society and working within the confines of already existing culture.[24]

Elsewhere, there was a similar programme in New York City:

> Rent is a major source of profits ... the biggest local industry. Meanwhile, NYC's redoubtable social housing programmes have been gutted. Rent

regulations have been rolled back almost entirely. The baseline cost of living is incredibly high. Hope? Well, for artists, there is some. What New York City does have is a set of regulated programs whereby the city government and private landlords, acting through cultural agencies, make a small sliver of the city's vast reservoir of vacant spaces available to artists and other cultural workers on a short-term basis. Agreements for artists to use vacant city-owned properties in areas deemed ripe for urban renewal began during the 1960s.[25]

We might also point to the infamous Christiania squat in Copenhagen, an empty military base that was occupied in the late 1960s and which could be described as 'an artist town … one big cultural workshop, which helps to fill the cultural void of contemporary Denmark.'[26] Christiania has been through various phases of property relations, including being squatted, threatened with eviction, criminalised and stigmatised as a drug market, and paying rent to the city, before eventually being purchased by the community itself. There's also the Gangeviertel squat in Hamburg, where squatters even made strategic references to creative city policies in order to stall eviction, declaring in a 2009 press conference that 'we are helping you to reach your goals facilitating a creative city of talent – here we are, with a cultural programme and a space; we are many and multiplying.'[27]

In Paris, different ideological stances on negotiation have caused a split between 'artistic' and 'anarchist' squats, which has been easily exploited by the city authorities who can divide them into different 'types' of 'good and bad', 'legitimate and illegitimate' squatter. 'Artistic squats', argues Verdier:

distinguish themselves from anarchists by claiming their specialisation and their title, but especially because some of them decided not to take any political stand. This led to a separation between collectives who claim illegality as a means to build the conditions of a social war, a political and cultural revolution, and those who try to normalise their situation in order to build stable workshops and galleries.[28]

The city's proactive policy towards artistic squats, which sought to legalise occupations with 'meanwhile' use agreements, also forced conditions on those crews to produce activity reports, financial statements, ensure a rotation of people in the space, and organise entertainment and cultural activities within their neighbourhood.[29]

And yet the reason squats are coopted by creative cities is because, despite contributing to the city's wider urban vibrancy, they sit on the margins of mainstream culture. In the UK, there are many examples of now-celebrated artists who began their careers in these spaces. Sculptor and artist Anthony Gormley made an impassioned plea in defence of squatting in the run-up to criminalisation in 2012, arguing that 'squatting is a very good way of preserving properties while at the same time putting them to good use ... it's a no-brainer that properties that are awaiting renovation or don't have commercial tenants can be of use for creative things, and indeed to provide shelter for the homeless'.[30] Gormley himself, as an art student, had squatted for six years in a factory in King's Cross in the 1970s, as part of an artist community that used the space.

Probably the most renowned and successful squatters, however, are The Clash. The band were originally called 'The 101ers' after 101 Walterton Road, the building they squatted in Maida Vale and which was just round the corner from Elgin Avenue (the row of houses squatted by Jeremy Corbyn's brother Piers, and who managed to successfully formalise their use of the building). Other musicians connected to squatting include the Sex Pistols' Johnny Rotten and Sid Vicious, who reportedly squatted the New Court building in Hampstead (now a £5 million block of flats), as well as Depeche Mode, Scritti Politti, My Bloody Valentine, Stereolab, and The Levellers.[31] In an interview with Virgin Radio, Bob Geldof of Boomtown Rats and Live Aid fame, revealed that when he first moved to London from Ireland, he was initially living on the streets, but later moved into a squat:

You're very young, you're 19, there's nothing going for you, you don't think anything is going to happen. I just had to keep moving. Just keep moving. Something will happen to you. It's going to be okay. Something, something one day will happen. And it did.[32]

Other notable squatters include Sting, Mark Knopfler (Dire Straits) and Richard Branson (who lived in the basement of a London house owned by the parents of a friend in 1967–8).[33] When Annie Lennox and Dave Stewart cofounded The Eurythmics in the late 1970s, they also needed space to set up a home studio and experiment with new technologies such as synthesisers, drum machines, and 4-track recorders. Lennox revealed, in a speech to the Royal Academy of Music, that she had 'passed through a series of cheap rooms, bed sits and flats ranging across several London boroughs' while supporting herself 'with a variety of part time jobs', and had been on the verge of 'packing up and going back to Scotland' before squatting a small space above a record store in Crouch End, London. Lennox told the audience that she persisted, despite her housing situation, because music was crucial, with its ability 'to inspire, to soothe, to heal, to celebrate, to connect and humanise us ... music has the power to do these things. All you have to do is bring it forth.'[34]

Finally, we might point to the cultural importance of a series of squats which sprang up around Tottenham Court Road and Euston Road in the late 1970s, inhabited by art students, DJs, musicians, and 'any other "outcasts" who felt at home in what sounds like the complete, non-stop chaos of the place'.[35] Boy George was part of a crew who squatted a five-story Edwardian residence here in the late 1970s/early 1980s, which reportedly 'still managed to look fabulous even without access to running water or a working toilet',[36] while the Warren Street Squat, occupied in 1978, facilitated the coming together of many cultural icons, including Leigh Bowery, Michael Clark, Stevie Stewart and David Holah, Princess Julia, and Mark Lebon (some of whom now have works displayed at the National Portrait Gallery).

Squats are sources and springs of social vitality. These emergent spaces *are* the city, not a threat to it. There needs to be far greater recognition of the cultural and democratic necessity of these spaces; but this is a form of respect which must not immediately push for formalisation via the ownership model, or facilitate surrender to the profit motives of capital. Skateboarders, graffiti artists, guerrilla gardeners, hawkers, rough sleepers, peddlers, Gypsy-Travellers, street dancers, buskers and performers ... these are examples of citizens using their city, avoiding the limited budgets or formal permissions required by bureaucracy, so that they might directly repurpose and reinhabit disused or wasted spaces. Instead of evicting or formalising (co-opting), public money could be made available to remove barriers to the survival of these spaces.

Rather than going along with austerity and 'big society' ideas that give up society to the whims of the market, local authorities could be more pro-active in supporting these spaces, but they should do so as enablers, not arbiters. Socially progressive urban policy would surely allow grounded initiatives to emerge, even providing public resources that might help spaces be safe, accessible, energy-efficient, maintained, and protected from the overheads of rent, insurance, and utilities, rather than wasting money on constant policing, eviction, or top-down programmes which presume, or try to anticipate, what the city wants or needs. Thought also needs to be given to how to hold back the tide of gentrification, which overcomes and suffocates community initiative. Like a snake swallowing its own tail, investment is bound to eat itself and destroy all that is characteristically creative and potentially inclusive about such projects. Yet the reason they are sought after in the first place is precisely because they are the pulse of vibrancy, of an exciting, creative, and provocative urban culture, of new horizons, aspirations, and ideas.

Conclusion: Nothing for Something

London in particular.
The town I've settled in.
Where definitions blur and the reaps of history are disinterred.
Where our spirits, driven, urgent, by the desire to finish first.
The big smoke.
I add my little cloud to it.

— Dizraeli, 'Strong Bright'

Squatting reveals the city of which it is a part. Squats continuously reperform the politics of property, confronting economic inequality and political disempowerment. Squatters push us to interrogate the urban: Why are there so many vacant buildings when people cannot access the spaces they need? Who can live, belong, or participate in the city, and who decides? Who are 'we' and what is 'our' vision for change? Where can we find spaces to imagine, be creative, and negotiate our different aspirations for space? As direct action, squatting is both a means and an end to addressing these questions. By intervening into the city, squatters reshape its buildings and alter its landscape, materially and socially. Spaces are made useful in cities that otherwise enclose and deny so many of us access, often only benefiting those with the power to own, or the wealth to lease. The state and the market are failing to offer people the resources they need, so squatters are taking the initiative. While the (dominant) ownership model of property conveniently denies or ignores questions of justice, each squat materialises the city's contradictions and puts social relations back on the table.

London is a city that has been taken over by the forces of capitalist markets. The pursuit of profit is acting as a barrier to space, prioritising return on investment over need. This is reflected both in the types of buildings being knocked down and erected, as well as the sheer extent of property being kept empty. Yet, as different experiences of housing crisis attest, the pursuit of safe and secure homes through the ownership model only perpetuates exclusion, inaccessibility, and injustice. Price and need have never been so far apart, yet the state has increasingly stepped away from any notion of social responsibility. Instead, the UK government has redoubled efforts to use criminal law to protect property and owners, targeting those marginalised by the very system they are championing, including squatters, but also rough sleepers, roadside Gypsies and Travellers, activists damaging monuments or infrastructure, ravers, and immigrants.

London is also a city where the state has asserted its 'ownership' of public spaces and buildings,[1] most notably social housing, in a way which has facilitated forces of social cleansing and gentrification. Centrifugal forces have been let loose upon homes and communities, spinning them away from their neighbourhoods and dislocating networks of care and belonging. Location is the name of the game for capital as developers seek to find and invest in new spaces for 'regeneration'. Rather than attempting to protect the right for existing users of the city to stay put, local authorities seem far more interested in facilitating market investment through planning permission, compulsory purchase orders, and (if it comes to it) eviction by force. The state considers itself mandated to turf people out of their homes, completely denying the use-claims of those who are already in those spaces, as crisis after crisis puts the squeeze on living standards.

Squats can be an eye in the storm and raise questions around who has the right to decide which people can take up space and not only be *located*, but also *participate*, in the city. As spaces of defiant domesticity, occupations at the Carpenters, Sweets Way, and Aylesbury estates, acted as anchor points and campaign spaces for individuals and communities to hang on, stay put, and stake their claim in the face of domicide. These are spaces which can allow not only an assertion of a 'right to the city', but also a radical squatter citizenship which creates its own basis for legitimacy and flies in the face of state definitions of borders, belonging, and participation. Some squats attempt to be explicitly proactive on social injustice issues. Whether setting up mutual aid networks during the COVID-19 pandemic, pay-what-you-will cafes and social spaces, or providing space to stay while waiting for an asylum application to go through, this book has shared examples where squatting is not only a lifeline but a space of care in an otherwise hostile environment.

Squats are spaces of solidarity for the marginalised and the ignored. They are another level before the street, a safety net below the safety net. Though rendered precarious by criminalisation, stigmatisation, and the material conditions of long-abandoned spaces, squats can be spaces of hope and immediate support. It's easy to dismiss squats as dangerous spaces, full of feckless hedonistic dropouts unwilling to contribute to the city and society. But such stereotypes rarely capture the truth on the ground, ignoring both the context and the sophistication of different uses of space, in favour of prejudiced narratives mobilised to justify more powers to protect owners. When the social safety net has been made threadbare by austerity, squats catch those who fall through the gaps, and yet they are being directly demonised for doing so.

Squats give people the space and time that the wage–rent vortex so often deprives us of. Housing crisis does not mean the same thing for everyone, but squats can allow for refuge from the freezing street just as much as they can allow for someone to find somewhere to live. As Streets Kitchen demonstrated at Sofia House, squats can be a lifeline. But as the accounts shared in this book show, others have found better mental health, community, belonging, and purpose, through squatting. When the options are between rough sleeping, sofa-surfing, getting a meaningless job (if you're able) just to pay extortionate rent on a poor-quality space, or moving back to the family home (if you're lucky), squatting offers choice.

Squats are used for multiple reasons and, while not always harmonious, they nevertheless allow for the disorder of contrasting use-claims to space. People can have different aspirations or visions for the same space, which often align with ideas of what they consider is *best* for society as a whole. But here, people can actually participate directly within contradictions. Squats are spaces of encounter and articulation but also, by the same token, 'zones of anticipation'.[2] By providing arenas for the negotiation of space, they are representative of wider conflicts over space across society. By providing infrastructure for grassroots democratic organisation, as well as for creativity and imagination, squats can play a central role enabling participation in social change. They are spaces of connection and communal gatherings, with the potential to support networks of affinity across the city.

In not being able (or willing) to assert ownership over a space, squat crews instead grapple directly with issues of inclusion or exclusion, and what criteria might be used to decide whether someone can use a space. Some, such as the Anarchist Nation of Autonomous Libertarians (ANAL), cope with questions of criteria by embracing the chaos and precarity of squatting, simply moving buildings when a space becomes untenable. But they can struggle to build this into anything before burnout sets in. Others have house meetings or trial periods for those wanting to join a space, while others still simply live only with people that they already know. Loose principles such as 'don't be a dickhead', referring to types such as 'vampires', or hierarchies of authenticity such as 'black underpants', are part of a wide-ranging set of norms which are drawn upon to guide property relations within squats. Yet operating through such vague guidelines potentially brings with it a lack of accountability and can play into unacknowledged hierarchies, particularly around class and gender. Some squats, however, do acknowledge and seek to deal with these issues directly as part of the politics of use, recognising that these are structures that disempower people and put limits on how they can use the space.

Squats can create infrastructure for articulation, discussion, and campaigns. They are centres where people can come together, learn, share, and organise. They are decentres which act as nodes, supporting networks across the city. As examples such as 56a, ASS, Sabaar bookshop/121 Centre, and the Rainbow Centres illustrate, these are symbolic hubs in the city. By housing counter-histories and community archives, they provide grassroots authority over space against powerful uprooting forces that either ignore such histories or seek to further repress them and what they represent.[3] While it can be difficult, given the stigma surrounding squats, to engage with wider publics, the ability for squats to act as campaign spaces crosses over with their material interventions into the city, allowing them to pick up on a wide range of issues such as housing, gentrification, capitalism, corruption, asylum/migrant solidarity, and the climate emergency. By providing material hubs and platforms, these spaces keep the need for change alive and have the potential to allow for direct participation from the ground up.

The legitimacy of squats, as well as any use of space, is socially constructed. Types and taxonomies play into these constructions, acting as a punitive discourse in which squatting can be stigmatised and outlawed, while ignoring the messiness of property use on the ground. Instead, a succession of artificial binaries – 'good'/'bad', 'deserving'/'undeserving', 'legitimate'/'illegitimate' – obscure the property norms that give rise to these judgements and constitute the groundwork for criminalisation and marginality. This framework denies the way that many of the problems faced by squatters, such as housing precarity, the inability to stay located in a city, the loss of social space for coming together to organise or find community and belonging, are created *by* this very property system.

In the end, stereotypes of squatters are simply reflections of legal and moral property norms which, as the comparison between the squatters in the military camps and those in the Duchess of Bedford House in 1946 demonstrated, change over time. They are discourses which extend, perpetuate, and seek to control ideas around what counts as proper or improper use of space, as well as legitimate or illegitimate users of space, informing media and political discourses which have helped to 'justify' criminalisation. In the run-up to the Criminal Law Act 1977, the Criminal Justice Act 1994, and the Legal Aid, Sentencing, and Punishment of Offenders Act 2012, the squatter stereotypes that were being peddled were remarkably similar. Each time, squatters were depicted as outsiders (whether through age, class, or ethnicity), lazy, weird, and on the fringes. They were also depicted as thieves directly threatening homeowners. Yet this has never been the intention of squatters, both practically, because you don't tend to last long in a property someone else is already using, and politically, because their aim is to recycle the empties. The slippage in these discourses, however, lets the ownership model off the hook. Squatting is presented as a threat to modest homes that are already being used by residents, while the power of property ownership to enclose and exclude people from vast swathes of the city is ignored.

The problem with using such types is that they do not allow for the recognition of nuance or the complexity of what is happening on the ground. As Kesia Reeve puts it, 'the complexity of squatting (the overlapping circumstances, concerns and goals of those involved, and the shifting cultural, political and housing contexts in which it takes place) prohibits a simplistic characterisation or typology of squatting.'[4] In their occupation of a space, squatters tread the line of property entitlement and challenge existing notions of 'who deserves what'. Squats can challenge what is considered to be legitimate use simultaneously on multiple fronts and in a single space. A squat can become a temporary home, as well as a social centre, and a place for work or creativity. These uses can come into conflict and lead to the dissolution of a particular squat or crew. But, once again, this simply demonstrates the potential of squats to allow for disagreement, conflict, negotiation, and compromise over their use. This is something that stands in direct contrast to the ownership model, which precisely attempts to avoid messy questions of social justice, in favour of systems which support the simple authority of the owner.

Squatting is an open door. Without ownership, squatters directly grapple with property relations of use on the ground. Judgements of legitimate or illegitimate use are *not* based upon an assertion of title, which means there is the potential for negotiation and compromise. There is more room for flexibility, contingency, conflict, and mutual agreement. In theory, no squatter can claim exclusive authority over a space, simply because they don't have recognised ownership of it, leaving open the possibility for a more inclusionary politics and ethics.

This book has shared examples of squatters in London who, forced by their precarious circumstances to try to find more ways to hold on to a space, have negotiated with landlords by offering free security in return for their ongoing use of the building and (later) an easy eviction. Crews are forced to navigate this context carefully, considering questions around whether to try to resist eviction, to seek informal negotiation, or (if on offer) formalisation through a city scheme. As well as through eviction, the ownership model can reassert and reperform itself through such moments of negotiation, by reconsolidating the authority of the owner over the user. As Heddy and others have found, negotiation between squatters and owners can be a strategic way to hold on to valuable spaces and maintain their longevity. Yet, as demonstrated by 'breeding places'-style programmes rolled out across many cities, as well as London's squatter amnesty in 1977, negotiation can also bring in elements of the ownership model which render the space precarious in other ways – liable for rent or a contract being cancelled. The introduction of the ownership model can also change property relations within the space, insofar as individuals now feel they have a stake to protect against others, or that they need to be more careful and controlling over the distribution of space for certain uses. Negotiation can also play into unequal distributions of space in the wider city. Selective permission allowing some squatting may, on the face of it, appear to be a proactive and logical step local authorities can take to make vacant spaces available for use (mostly by artists). But they can also play into creative city policies which turn squatters into shock troops for gentrification in parts of the city which 'require development'. Such state-sanctioned 'squatting' can also play into hierarchies of whose use is seen as legitimate – that is, the 'highest and best use' according to the agenda of the state or local authorities rather than the reality of use-needs on the ground.

The ownership model of property is oppressive, both historically and today, as it continues to deny any claims to space of non-owners. Such claims are pre-positioned as improper and illegitimate, drawing from a long history of binaries which equate the value of a person with their relationship to property. Property becomes depoliticised under the ownership model.[5] By positioning non-owners as savages, uncivilised, and inherently incapable of being able to maximise the value of a space, the way in which we currently frame property draws upon 'racial regimes of ownership',[6] which assume that all property relations are 'settled' in advance.[7] The echo of these narratives is still being put to use against property outlaws today, including through stereotypes of squatters. Yet, over time, the roots of this property logic in settler colonial violence and the civilising offensive[8] against indigenous uses of land have become obscured, allowing ownership to dominate the way in which we think about legitimate use and clouding the idea that there could be alternative ways to negotiate space in a more equitable and just manner.

There is a long and forgotten history of use-claims to space. From the one-night cottages, through to the London Squatters Campaign, squatters have drawn upon both customs and laws in order to legitimise and protect their ongoing use of a space. Adverse possession has a rocky precedent. It is a tool that was actively mobilised by settler colonial states to enclose 'unused' (i.e. indigenous) land. Contemporary uses of adverse possession have been undermined by the push for comprehensive land registration, and they can corrupt the flexibility of squats by bringing in elements of the ownership model, changing the relationship between people using a space. Yet the concept nevertheless points to a past where use was recognised as a legitimate claim to possession of a space.

Squatting is the championing of use of over ownership, but one which doesn't predetermine what or who counts as 'highest and best use'. As a form of trespass, squats open up the performativity of property on the ground. Ownership is *not* a pre-given and is something that must continually reassert itself, because 'property is always unstable … property regimes have to be constantly enacted and negotiated to be maintained; they are the result of social struggles'.[9] The aim of ownership is to clean up property relationships through titles, registers, maps and surveys, which delineate boundaries that should not be crossed. In this way, the ownership model actively restricts the possible uses which can exist within a space, as well as who or what is permissible where. It 'organizes the world for us, assigning resources to owners, apportioning rights and duties, constituting markets, organizing concepts of citizenship and political identity, and grounding dissent and protest'.[10] Simply by repurposing and reshaping a small corner of the city, squatters present a challenge to these pre-designations and (re)assert the importance of use over ownership.

Squatters highlight the shared importance of space. The fact that a space isn't being utilised should be considered a bigger social priority than finding new ways to protect owners. This is a point that squatters make, through their actions, again and again. Each squat is a microcosm of how space is being poorly distributed in relation to our diverse needs, because squatters need space for the same reasons as any of us. We need somewhere dry, warm, secure, and hygienic to sleep, eat, and keep clean. We need somewhere to feel cared for and to belong. We need to be located in a certain city or a particular part of the city. We need space to socialise as well as build and participate in communities. We need spaces in which to organise and platforms on which to be heard and seen. We need free time to pursue something other than wages or domestic labour. And all these needs do not exist in isolation, they overlap. Some people are pushed towards squatting because they're in a desperate housing situation, but they then use that space in diverse and life-affirming ways. After all, being 'homeless' is not an identity, nor does it mean the same for each individual, even if stereotypes around what it means to be homeless seek to reduce it to this. People use space for different purposes in varying circumstances and at different points in their life course, and squatters are no exception.

Squats are spaces which push the limits of imagination and possibility. They offer outlets for new ideas and experimentation, which not only contribute to the cultural vibrancy of the city but also open up possibilities for radical change. Squats are often dismissed as hedonistic or apolitical, but their importance as cultural and artistic hubs should be recognised. They can provide free time and space for 'non-profitable' but vital social activity, and serve as access points to creativity for those who would otherwise not have the means to engage in artistic activity. As a recent report from the Creative Industries Policy and Evidence Centre found, working-class people are under-represented in every area of arts and culture, with fewer than 1 in 10 arts workers in the UK coming from working-class roots.[11] As tools for expression, the ability to break through established tastes and economic limits on aesthetics using cultural tools of expression is inherently political, potentially providing the materials from which to affect others. Whether through the participatory values of Temporary Autonomous Art (TAA), the studio and exhibition spaces provided by squatting, or the communal experience of free parties or raves, art and culture provide material spaces for platforms, community, and solidarity.

By looking at London from the margins, we could reimagine the city. We could visualise a horizon which is not dominated by cold and empty luxury flats, or phallic skyscraper monuments to capital, and instead go beyond the distribution of space in the city created by the ownership model. We might instead recognise the right of people to stay put in the city, or to come to the city to participate in diverse ways, which exist beyond state designations of legitimate or illegitimate citizens in the urban landscape. By allowing grassroots infrastructure to persist, perhaps we could also imagine London as a space that allows for voice, creativity, and community organisations, which can thrive without immediately trying to incorporate them into corrupting systems of ownership.

This book does not paint a complete picture of London, let alone of squatting in general. London is just one major city, but squatting is of international significance. The United Nations estimates there are 1 billion squatters on the planet, 10 per cent of the world's population living, working, creating, and *using* spaces they do not own or have permission to use.[12] More people are living in cities now than are not and, as urbanisation continues, people are using squatting to find the spaces they need. While often marginalised, in poor condition, and politically ignored, these urban corners *are* the city in action. These settlements are precarious, stigmatised, and criminalised, but they are also safety nets; anchors to stay located and participate in the city; spaces of care, social reproduction, and solidarity; platforms for articulation and organising; as well as creative, imaginative, and generative spaces.

In *For the City Yet to Come*, Simone observes that African cities are often portrayed as 'not working' or 'works in progress' in comparison with 'Western' cities, with urban Africans depicted as 'reluctant participants in urbanisation'.[13] This comes from a perspective which positions cities in the 'global South' as inherently and characteristically informal, chaotic, underdeveloped, and corrupt. But not only is this a perspective based upon Enlightenment notions which place European 'civilisation' as superior, it also incorrectly frames cities in 'the North' or 'the West' as formal and ordered in comparison. It is also a limited perspective, because it can't help but overlook the 'enormous creative energies' of informal spaces, which 'have been ignored, squandered, and left unused'.[14] Instead of emphasising the need for development or the intervention of formal institutions, Simone argues that we need to focus on 'a wide range of diffuse experimentation', the importance of 'ambiguities'[15] and the possibilities of urban 'becoming' which are opened up by auto-constructed and self-constituted spaces and networks. For Simone, we need to recognise the importance of those activities which make use of a city, in terms of:

> the conjunction of seemingly endless possibilities of remaking … with its artifice of architectures, infrastructures, and sedimentation channelling movement, transaction, and physical proximity, bodies constantly 'on the line' to affect and be affected, 'delivered up' to specific terrain and possibilities of recognition or coalescence.[16]

It would be lazy and problematic to simply draw equivalences or comparisons between squatting in London and diverse urban experiences across distinct African cities such as Dakar, Pretoria, and Douala. But what we might take from this is a lesson on the importance of 'in-between' spaces for urban life. Rather than being seen as spaces which signal the failure of the city, or limits to its success, liminal spaces can in fact be *generative* of 'imagination and well-being, of making links and operating in concert with the larger world', meaning that we need to 'amplify the sensibility, creativity, and rationality of everyday practices and behaviours that either are invisible or appear strange',[17] or even 'heretical'.[18]

Others have also pointed to the importance of marginalised and informalised spaces as *generative*. It is certainly true that fragmented urban life may take place within a context of precarity and risk, yet 'social collectives working with broken down or inadequate buildings, infrastructures or community provisions' contain within them 'rhythms of maintenance, improvisation, incremental improvement and the often gendered labour of holding things together even as they break down and fall apart'.[19] If formality, on the one hand, 'operates through the fixing of value, including the mapping of spatial value', then what is simultaneously liberatory and precarious about informality, is that it 'operates through the constant negotiability of value and the unmapping of space'.[20] Informality allows the value of a space to be continually re-imagined and contested.

In many different cities and contexts, people making use of space in ways that fall beyond the recognition of the state or the market, are treated as 'other' and not part of the 'normal' city'; and yet urban forms such as the 'favela', 'slum', and 'barrio' (i.e. 'squatter settlements') are in reality 'an extremely functional solution to many of the problems faced by its residents ... [providing] access to jobs and services, a tightly knit community in which reciprocal favours ... [mitigate] hardships, and above all, free housing'.[21] While such transnational comparisons must avoid the trap of invoking what Spivak calls the 'authenticity of the other', what they can allow us to do is reframe, recontextualise, and reconsider squatting in cities like London, by re-examining 'the processes through which geopolitical realities are constructed and depicted'.[22] However, as Yiftachl and Yakobi point out, informality is also 'a form of social control' insofar as it also allows urban elites to represent themselves as 'open, civil and democratic, whilst at the same time denying great numbers of urban residents and workers basic rights and services'.[23] The history of squatting – as well as other controversial uses of space such as sex shows, prostitution, and safe drug use – being incorporated into urban policies that present a city as 'tolerant' and 'innovative' speaks to this.[24]

Squats *are* part of the city, not separated from it, and they have implications for the urban as a whole. Squatters are users of property. They make rival moral claims to space that jar with formal property systems. However, as property users, they also enter into property relations with owners (landlords, police, security, neighbours) as well as each other. Rather than scroungers wanting 'something for nothing', however, we would be better off considering squats as an example of turning 'nothing into something'. Squatters are an example of an efficient and direct creation of material and social infrastructure, offering spaces of care and nodes of solidarity, in the context of social cleansing, un-homing, dispossession, austerity, a broken safety net, and a hostile environment. Squats are spaces of insurgency, convergence, and collectivity. They provide people with the opportunity to be part of something bigger than themselves. A chance to find space and time. To be generative and creative. To be non-profitable. And a platform from which to speak and be seen. These are affective and effective spaces of solidarity.

Notes

INTRODUCTION: THE LONDON UNDERGROUND

1. Fox O'Mahony, L., O'Mahony. D. and Hickey, R. 2015. Introduction – Criminalising squatting: Setting an agenda. In L. Fox O'Mahony, D. O'Mahony and R. Hickey (eds) *Moral Rhetoric and the Criminalisation of Squatting: Vulnerable Demons?* Abingdon: Routledge, pp. 4–5.

2. Penalver, E. and Katyal, S. 2010. *Property Outlaws: How Squatter Pirates, and Protestors Improve the Law of Ownership.* Newhaven, CT: Yale University Press.

3. Dee, E.T.C. 2013. Moving towards criminalisation and then what? In Squatting Europe Kollective (eds) *Squatting in Europe: Radical Spaces, Urban Struggles.* New York: Minor Compositions, p. 263.

4. Grohmann, S. 2017. Space invaders: The 'migrant squatter' as the ultimate intruder. In P. Mudu and S. Chatoopadhay (eds) *Migration, Squatting and Radical Autonomy.* Abingdon: Routledge, p. 124.

5. Watson, D. 2016. *Squatting in Britain 1945–1955: Housing, Politics and Direct Action.* Milton Keynes: Merlin Press, p. 70.

6. Ibid. p. 71.

7. Ibid. p. 94.

8. Webber, H. 2012. A domestic rebellion: The squatters' movement of 1946. *Ex Historia* 4, 125–46.

9. Burgum, S. 2019. From Grenfell Tower to the Home Front: Unsettling property norms using a genealogical approach. *Antipode* 51(2), 458–77.

10. Mudu, P. 2013. Resisting and challenging neoliberalism: The development of Italian social centres. In Squatting Europe Kollective (eds) *Squatting in Europe: Radical Spaces, Urban Struggles.* New York: Minor Compositions, p. 68.

11. Watson, *Squatting in Britain 1945–1955*, p. 101.

12. Ward, C. 1980. *Cotters and Squatters: The Hidden History of Housing.* Nottingham: Five Leaves, p. 104.

13. Ibid. p. 43.

14. Ibid. p. 31.

15. Ibid. p. 107

16. Ibid. p. 113.

17. Bailey, R. 1973. *The Squatters.* London: Penguin.

18. Ibid. p. 65.

19. Finchett-Maddock, L. 2016. *Protest, Property and the Commons: Performances of Law and Resistance.* Abingdon: Routledge, p. 48.

20. Platt, S. 1980. A decade of squatting: The story of squatting in Britain since 1968. In N. Wates and C. Wolmar (eds) *Squatting: The Real Story.* London: Bay Leaf Books, p. 21.

21. Grohman, S. 2019. *The Ethics of Space: Homelessness and Squatting in Urban England*. Chicago: HAU Books, p. 10.
22. Finchett-Maddock, L. 2015. The changing architecture of adverse possession and a political aesthetics of squatting. In O'Mahony et al. (eds), *Moral Rhetoric and the Criminalisation of Squatting*, p. 213.
23. Fox O'Mahony et al., Introduction – Criminalising squatting, p. 1.
24. Ibid. p. 53.
25. Wates, N. 1976. *The Battle for Tolmers Square*. Abingdon: Routledge, p. 180.
26. Ibid. p. 26.
27. Finchett-Maddock, The changing architecture of adverse possession.
28. Waring, E. 2015. Adverse possession: Relativity to absolutism. In O'Mahony et al. (eds) *Moral Rhetoric and the Criminalisation of Squatting*, p. 182.
29. Ward, C. 1980. The early squatters. In N. Wates and C. Wolmar, *Squatting: The Real Story*. London: Bay Leaf Books, p. 109.
30. Finchett-Maddock, L. 2014. Squatting in London: Squatters' rights and legal movement(s). In B. van der Steen and A. Katzeff (eds) *The City is Ours*. Oakland, CA: PM Press, p. 211.
31. Fennell, L.A. 2006. Efficient trespass: The case for 'bad faith' adverse possession. 100 *Northwestern University Law Review*, 1037.
32. Cockburn, P., Bruun, M., Risager, B. and Thorup, M. 2018. Introduction: Disagreement as a window onto property. In M.H. Bruun, P.J.L. Cockburn, B.S. Risager and M. Thorup (eds) *Contested Property Claims: What Disagreement Tells Us about Ownership*. Abingdon: Routledge, p. 2.
33. Starecheski, A. 2016. *Ours to Lose: When Squatters Became Homeowners in New York City*. Chicago: University of Chicago Press, p. 21.
34. Ibid. p. 22.
35. Singer, J. 2000. *Entiitlement: The Paradoxes of Property*. Newhaven, CT: Yale University Press.
36. Blomley, N. 2005. Remember property? *Progress in Human Geography* 29(2), 125.
37. Ibid. p. 127.
38. Bhandar, B. 2018. *Colonial Lives of Property: Law, Land, and Racial Regimes of Ownership*. Durham, NC: Duke University Press, p. 181.
39. Griffin, C. 2023. Enclosure as internal colonisation: The subaltern commoner. *Terra Nullius* and the settling of England's 'wastes'. *Transactions of the Royal Historical Society* 1, 95–120.
40. Noterman, E. 2022. Adverse commoning: Tracing contested legal geographies of urban commons. *Environment and Planning D: Society and Space* 40(1), 99.
41. Ibid. p. 101.
42. Ibid. p. 103.
43. Starecheski, *Ours to Lose*, p. 261.
44. Ibid. p. 190.
45. Ibid. p. 170.
46. Ibid. p. 94.

47. Action on Empty Homes. 2023. Regional Breakdown: London. https://static1. squarespace.com/static/6553693f7d629a133b6a4ece/t/6556395f5ebbf5732fcbc 36e/1700149600422/London+stats.pdf

48. Office of National Statistics. 2023. Number of vacant and second homes in England. www.ons.gov.uk/peoplepopulationandcommunity/housing/bulletins/ numberofvacantandsecondhomesenglandandwales/census2021

49. Burgum, S. and Vasudevan, A. 2023. Critical geographies of occupation, squatting, and trespass. *City* 27(3–4), 354.

50. Lancione, M. 2019. Weird exoskeletons: Propositional politics and the making of home in underground Bucharest. *International Journal of Urban and Regional Research* 43(3), 535–50.

51. Simone, A. 2004. *For The City Yet to Come: Changing African Life in Four Cities.* Durham, NC: Duke University Press.

52. Burgum and Vasudevan, Critical geographies of occupation, 352.

53. Lewis, P. and Evans, R. 2013. *Undercover: The True Story of Britain's Secret Police.* London: Guardian Faber Publishing.

54. Atkinson, R. and Jacobs, K. 2016. *House, Home and Society.* Oxford: Palgrave Macmillan, p. 157.

55. Ibid. p. 157.

56. Ibid. p. 159.

SOLIDARITY ON GREAT PORTLAND STREET

1. Maestri, G. and Monforte, P. 2024. Victims and agents: The representation of refugees among British volunteers active in the refugee support sector. In S. Burgum and K. Higgins (eds) *How the Other Half Lives: Interconnecting Socio-spatial Inequalities.* Manchester: Manchester University Press.

1. THESE PEOPLE NEED HOMES, THESE HOMES NEED PEOPLE

1. Dorling, D. 2014. *All that Is Solid: How the Great Housing Disaster Defines Our Times, and What We Can Do about It.* London: Allen Lane, p. 31.

2. Office for National Statistics. 2023. Number of vacant and second homes in England and Wales. www.ons.gov.uk/peoplepopulationandcommunity/ housing/bulletins/numberofvacantandsecondhomesenglandandwales/ census2021

3. UK Gov. 2023. Ending rough sleeping data framework. September 2023. www. gov.uk/government/publications/ending-rough-sleeping-data-framework-september-2023/ending-rough-sleeping-data-framework-september-2023

4. *The Big Issue.* 2023. How many people are homeless in the UK. www.bigissue. com/news/housing/how-many-people-are-homeless-in-the-uk-and-what-can-you-do-about-it/

5. Madden, D. and Marcuse, P. 2016. *In Defence of Housing: The Politics of Crisis.* London: Verso, p. 11.

6. Ibid. p. 11.
7. Ibid. p. 9.
8. Lancione, M. 2023. *For a Liberatory Politics of Home*. Durham, NC: Duke University Press, p. 11.
9. Ibid. pp. 3–4.
10. Madden, D. and Marcuse, P. 2016. *In Defence of Housing: The Politics of Crisis*. London: Verso, pp. 16–17.
11. Atkinson, R. and Blandy, S. 2016. *Domestic Fortress: Fear and the New Home Front*. Manchester: Manchester University Press, p. 8.
12. Minton, A. 2017. *Big Capital: Who is London For?* London: Penguin, p. xvi.
13. Ibid. p. 1.
14. Action on Empty Homes. 2023. *Empty Homes: How They Can Help Us Reach Net Zero*. Report. https://static1.squarespace.com/static/6553693f7d629a133b6a4ece/t/66068abf0a61b678c6e93c3c/1711704771108/howtheyhelpus.pdf
15. Dorling, D. 2014. *All That Is Solid: How the Great Housing Disaster Defines Our Times, and What We Can Do about It*. London: Allen Lane, p. 295.
16. Jacobs, K. 2019. *Neoliberal Housing Policy: An International Perspective*. Abingdon: Routledge, p. 95.
17. Ibid. p. 18.
18. Penny, J. 2024. Austerity and the local state: Governing and politicising 'actually existing austerity' in a post-democratic city. In Burgum and Higgins (eds) *How the Other Half Lives*.
19. Ibid. p. 51.
20. Lancione, *For a Liberatory Politics of Home*, p. 5.
21. Ward in ibid. p. 18.
22. Ibid. p. 18.
23. Freeman, J. 1972. The tyranny of structurelessness. *Berkeley Journal of Sociology* 17, 151–64.
24. Owens, L. 2013. Have squat will travel. In Squatting in Europe Kollective (eds) *Squatting in Europe: Radical Spaces, Urban Struggles*. New York: Minor Compositions, p. 190.
25. Ibid. p. 204.
26. Vasudevan, A. 2015. *The Autonomous City: A History of Urban Squatting*. London: Verso, p. 7.
27. Manjikian, M. 2013. *Securitization of Property Squatting in Europe*. Abingdon: Routledge, p. 8.
28. Ibid. p. 14.
29. Ibid. p. 31.
30. Atkinson, R. and Jacobs, K. 2016. *House, Home and Society*. Oxford: Palgrave Macmillan, p. 21.
31. Madden and Marcuse, *In Defence of Housing*, p. 68.
32. Atkinson, R. and Jacobs, K. 2016. *House, Home and Society*. Oxford: Palgrave Macmillan, p. 72.
33. Madden and Marcuse, *In Defence of Housing*, p. 64.

2. THE POLITICS OF LOCATION, THE LOCATION OF POLITICS

1. Bhandar, B. 2018. *Colonial Lives of Property: Law, Land, and Racial Regimes of Ownership*. Durham, NC: Duke University Press.

2. Begum, S. 2023. *From Sylhet to Spitalfields: Bengali Squatters in 1970s East London*. London: Lawrence & Wishart, p. 14.

3. Ibid. p. 81.

4. Squire, V. and Darling, J. 2013. The 'minor' politics of rightful presence: Justice and relationality in city of sanctuary. *International Political Sociology* 7(1), 59–74.

5. Begum, *From Sylhet to Spitalfields*, pp. 16–17.

6. Lefebvre, in Merrifield, A. 2011. The right to the city and beyond: Notes on a Lefebvrian re-conceptualisation. *CITY* 15(3–4), 475.

7. Vasudevan, A. 2015. *The Autonomous City: A History of Urban Squatting*. London: Verso, p. 243.

8. Ibid. p.151.

9. Dadusc, D., Grazioli, M. and Martinez, M. 2019. Introduction: citizenship as inhabitance? Migrant housing squats versus institutional accommodation. *Citizenship Studies* 23(6), 521–39.

10. de Carli, B. and Frediani, A. 2016. Insurgent regeneration: Spatial practices of citizenship in the rehabilitation of inner-city São Paulo. *GeoHumanities* 2(2), 335.

11. Darling, D. 2017. Acts, ambiguities, and the labour of contesting citizenship. *Citizenship Studies* 21(6), 727–36.

12. Maestri, G. and Hughes, S. 2017. Contested spaces of citizenship: Camps, borders, and urban encounters. *Citizenship Studies* 21(6), 626.

13. Darling, Acts, ambiguities, and the labour of contesting citizenship, 729.

14. Canepari, E. and Rosa, E. 2017. A quiet calm to citizenship: Mobility, urban spaces and city practices over time. *Citizenship Studies* 21(6), 658.

15. Dadusc et al., Introduction: citizenship as inhabitance?, 2.

16. Holston, J. 2009. *Insurgent Citizenship: Disjunctions of Democracy and Modernity in Brazil*. Princeton, NJ: Princeton University Press, p. 274.

17. Hardoy, J. and Satterthwaite, D. 1989. *Squatter Citizen: Life in the Urban Third World*. Abingdon: Routledge.

18. Ibid. pp. 15–17.

19. Holston, J. 2009. *Insurgent Citizenship: Disjunctions of Democracy and Modernity in Brazil*. Princeton, NJ: Princeton University Press, p. 4.

20. Ibid. p. 6.

21. Satterthwaite, D. and Mitlin, D. 2004. *Empowering Squatter Citizen: Local Government, Civil Society and Urban Poverty Reduction*. Abingdon: Routledge, p. 11.

22. Sparks, T. 2016. Citizens without property: Informality and political agency in a Seattle, Washington homeless encampment. *Environment and Planning A: Economy and Space* 49(1), 91–2.

23. de Carli, B. and Frediani, A. 2016. Insurgent regeneration: Spatial practices of citizenship in the rehabilitation of inner-city São Paulo. *GeoHumanities* 2(2), 341.

24. Atkinson, R. 2008. The great cut: The support for private modes of social evasion by public policy. *Social Policy and Administration* 42(6), 601.

25. Ibid. p. 603.

26. Milligan, R. 2023. Cracking buildings, cracking capitalism: Antagonism, affect, and the importance of squatting for housing justice. *CITY* 27(3–4), 416.

27. Gillespie, T., Hardy, K. and Watt, P. 2018. Austerity urbanism and Olympic counter-legacies: Gendering, defending and expanding the urban commons in East London. *Environment and Planning D: Society and Space* 36(5), 812.

28. Peck, J. 2012. Austerity urbanism: American cities under extreme economy. *CITY* 16(6), 26–55.

29. Watt, P. and Minton, A. 2016. London's housing crisis and its activisms. *CITY* 20(2), 204–21.

30. Gillespie et al. Austerity urbanism and Olympic counter-legacies, 825.

31. Tyler, I. 2013. *Revolting Subjects: Social Abjection and Resistance in Neoliberal Britain*. London: Zed Books, p. 159.

32. Milligan, Cracking buildings, cracking capitalism, 425.

33. Ibid. p. 422.

34. Ibid. p. 428.

35. 'Deptford square' refers to the corner of Deptford High Street and Giffin Street.

36. Darling, J. 2011. Domopolitics, governmentality and the regulation of asylum accommodation. *Political Geography* 30(5), 263–71.

37. Jones, H., Gunaratnam, Y., Bhattacharyya, G., Davies, W., Dhaliwal, S., Forkert, K. et al. 2017. *Go Home? The Politics of Immigration Controversies*. Manchester: Manchester University Press.

38. Cattaneo, C. 2013. Urban squatting, rural squatting and the ecological-economic perspective. In Squatting Europe Kollective (eds) *Squatting in Europe: Radical Spaces, Urban Struggles*. New York: Minor Compositions, p. 157.

39. Squire, V. and Darling, J. 2013. The 'minor' politics of rightful presence: Justice and relationality in city of sanctuary. *International Political Sociology* 7(1), 59–74.

40. Madden, D. and Marcuse, P. 2016. *In Defence of Housing: The Politics of Crisis*. London: Verso, p. 198.

41. Atkinson, R. 2008. The great cut: The support for private modes of social evasion by public policy. *Social Policy and Administration* 42(6), 602.

42. Elliott-Cooper, A., Hubbard, P. and Lees, L. 2019. Moving beyond Marcuse: Gentrification, displacement and the violence of un-homing. *Progress in Human Geography* 44(3), 492–509.

43. Minton, A. 2017. *Big Capital: Who is London For?* London: Penguin, pp. 49–50.

44. Elliott-Cooper et al. 2019. Moving beyond Marcuse, 504.

45. Ferreri, M. 2020. Painted bullet holes and broken promises: Understanding and challenging municipal dispossession in London's public housing 'decanting'. *International Journal of Urban and Regional Research* 44(6), 1007.

46. Ibid. p. 1008.

47. Ibid. p. 1009.
48. Roy, A. 2017. Dis/possessive collectivism: Property and personhood at city's end. *Geoforum* 80, A1–A11.
49. Van Isacker, T. 2019. Bordering through domicide: Spatializing citizenship in Calais. *Citizenship Studies* 23(6), 7.
50. Ibid. p. 4.
51. Roy, A. 2003. Paradigms of propertied citizenship: Transnational techniques of analysis. *Urban Affairs Review* 38(4), 463–91.
52. Harris, C. 1993. Whiteness as property. *Harvard Law Review* 106(8), 1707–91.
53. Hardoy, J. and Satterthwaite, D. 1989. *Squatter Citizen: Life in the Urban Third World*. Abingdon: Routledge, p. 24.

3. AN ASPIRATION FOR SPACE, A SPACE FOR ASPIRATION

1. Rao, V. 2009. Embracing urbanism: The city as archive. *New Literary History* 40(2), 380.
2. Wright-Mills, C. 1999. *The Sociological Imagination*. Oxford: Oxford University Press.
3. Rancière, J. 2010. *Dissensus: On Politics and Aesthetics*. London: Bloomsbury.
4. Dee, E.T.C. 2016. Squatted social centres in London: Temporary nodes of resistance to capitalism. *Contention: The Multidisciplinary Journal of Social Protest* 4(1–2), 110.
5. Mudu, P. 2004. Resisting and challenging neoliberalism: The development of Italian social centres. *Antipode* 36(5), 918.
6. Ibid. p. 918.
7. Piazza, G. 2016. Squatting social centres in a Sicilian city: Liberated spaces and urban protest actors. *Antipode* 50(2), 499.
8. Piazza, G. 2016. Squatting social centres in a Sicilian city: Liberated spaces and urban protest actors. *Antipode* 50(2), 498.
9. Wall, C. 2017. Sisterhood and squatting in the 1970s: Feminism, housing and urban change in Hackney. *History Workshop Journal* 83(1), 83.
10. Ibid. p. 90.
11. Ibid. p. 83.
12. Cook, M. 2013. 'Gay times': Identity, locality, memory, and the Brixton squats in 1970s London. *Twentieth Century British History* 24(1), 87.
13. Ibid. p. 87.
14. Ibid. p. 91.
15. Miller, M. 2023. 'We kind of created our own scene': A geography of the Brixton Rebel Dykes. *CITY* 27(3–4), p. 435.
16. Ibid. p. 438.
17. Ibid. p. 433.
18. Ibid. p. 442.
19. Remembering Olive Collective. 2007. Sabaar bookshop. https://remember olivemorris.wordpress.com/2007/09/26/sabaar-bookshop/
20. Beckles, C. 1998. 'We shall not be terrorised out of existence': The political legacy of England's Black bookshops. *Journal of Black Studies* 29(1), 51–72.

21. Past Tense. 2019. Today in London anarchist history 1999: The 121 Centre evicted, Brixton. https://pasttense.co.uk/2019/08/12/today-in-london-anarchist-history-1999-the-121-centre-evicted-brixton/comment-page-1/

22. Aguilera, T. 2018. The squatting movement(s) in Paris: Internal divides and conditions for survival. In M.A. Martínez López (ed.) *The Urban Politics of Squatters' Movements*. Oxford: Palgrave Macmillan.

23. Mudu, P. and Rossini, L. 2018. Occupations of housing and social centres in Rome: A durable resistance to neoliberalism and institutionalisation. In Martínez López (ed.) *The Urban Politics of Squatters' Movements*, p. 108.

24. Uitermark, J. 2004. The co-optation of squatters in Amsterdam and the emergence of a movement meritocracy: A critical reply to Pruijt. *International Journal of Urban and Regional Research* 28(3), 687–98.

25. Cattaneo, C. and Martínez, M. 2014. Introduction: Squatting as an alternative to capitalism. In Squatting Europe Kollective (ed.) *The Squatters' Movement in Europe: Commons and Autonomy as Alternatives to Capitalism*. London: Pluto Press, p. 5.

26. Ibid. p. 3.

27. Ibid. p. 27.

28. Ibid. p. 283.

29. González, R., Diáz-Parra, I. and Martínez-López, M. 2018. Squatted social centres and the housing question. In Martínez López (ed.) *The Urban Politics of Squatters' Movements*, p. 284.

30. Graeber, D. 2009. *Direct Action: An Ethnography*. London: AK Press, p. 107.

4. MAKING ROOM FOR ART, THE ART OF MAKING ROOM

1. Maffesoli, M. 1996. *The Time of The Tribes: The Decline of Individualism in Mass Society*. London: Sage.

2. Riley, S., Morey, Y. and Griffin, C. 2010. The 'pleasure citizen': Analysing partying as a form of social and political participation. *Young: Nordic Journal of Youth Research* 18(1), 37.

3. Ibid. p. 43.

4. Martin, D. 1999. Power play and party politics: The significance of raving. *Journal of Popular Culture* 32(4), 93–4.

5. Mujinga. 2015. Squatting in media/media in squatting. In A. Moore and A. Smart (eds) *Making Room: Cultural Production in Occupied Spaces*. Chicago: Other Forms, p. 342.

6. Bearder, P. 2019. *Stage Invasion: Poetry and the Spoken Word Renaissance*. London: Outspoken Press, p. 267.

7. Ibid. p. 279.

8. Ibid. p. 284.

9. Rancière, J. 2013. *The Politics of Aesthetics: The Distribution of the Sensible*. London: Bloomsbury, p. 8.

10. Davis, O. 2013. The politics of art: Aesthetic contingency and the aesthetic affect. In O. Davis (ed.) *Rancière Now: Current Perspectives on Jacques Rancière*. Oxford: Wiley Blackwell, p. 160.

11. Rancière, J. 2011. *The Emancipated Spectator*. London: Verso.
12. Davis, O. 2010. *Jacques Rancière*. Cambridge: Polity Press, p. 155.
13. Rancière in Marshall, B. 2013. Rancière and Deleuze: Entanglements of film theory. In Davis (ed.) *Rancière Now*, p. 174.
14. Davis, *Jacques Rancière*, p. 154.
15. Moore, A. 2015. Whether you like it or not. In Moore and Smart (eds) *Making Room*, p. 13.
16. Ibid. p. 13.
17. Jacobs, J. 2000. *The Death and Life of Great American Cities*. London: Pimlico, p. 200.
18. Ibid. p. 200.
19. Ibid. p. 201.
20. Ibid. p. 201.
21. Landry, C. 2006. *The Art of City Making*. Abingdon: Routledge.
22. Buchholz, T. 2015. Creativity and the capitalist city. In Moore and Smart (eds) *Making Room*, p. 44.
23. Boschma, V. 2015. The Autonomous Zone (de Vrije Ruimte). In Moore and Smart (eds) *Making Room*, p. 56.
24. Ibid. p. 56.
25. Moore, A. 2015. *Occupation Culture: Art and Squatting in the City from Below*. New York: Minor Compositions, p. 246.
26. Lillesoe, B. 2015. Christiania art and culture. In Moore and Smart (eds) *Making Room*, p. 96.
27. Fraeser, N. 2015. Gangeviertel, Hamburg. In Moore and Smart (eds) *Making Room*, p. 173.
28. Verdier, M. 2015. Situationism and its Influence on French Anarchist squats. In Moore and Smart (eds) *Making Room*, p. 223.
29. Prieur, V. 2015. Emergence and institutional recognition of artistic squats in Paris. In Moore and Smart (eds) *Making Room*.
30. *The Guardian*. 2012. Antony Gormley: Don't criminalise squatting, 31 Jan. www.theguardian.com/artanddesign/2012/jan/31/antony-gormley-dont-criminalise-squatting
31. Loben, C. 2011. Squats bred some of the best UK music – the Tories want to shut them down. https://louderthanwar.com/squats-bred-some-of-the-best-uk-music-the-tories-want-to-end-them/
32. Virgin Radio. 2021. Bob Geldof on turning 70. https://virginradio.co.uk/the-chris-evans-breakfast-show/35673/bob-geldof-on-turning-70-and-the-upcoming-boomtown-rats-live-shows
33. *The Guardian*. 1999. Famous faces who took rent-free route, 21 July. www.theguardian.com/uk/1999/jul/21/3
34. Lennox, A. 2017. Read Online: Annie's Royal Academy of Music acceptance speech. www.annielennox.com/read-online-annies-royal-academy-music-acceptance-speech/
35. Holt, B. 2012. The Warren Street squat: 80s club life with Boy George, Stephen Jones and many more. https://highereducationdegree-magha.blogspot.com/2012/04/the-warren-street-squat-80s-club-life.html

36. Myers, B. 2012. Criminalising squatters will hurt British pop music. *The Guardian*, 3 Sept. www.theguardian.com/music/musicblog/2012/se

CONCLUSION: NOTHING FOR SOMETHING

1. Christophers, B. 2018. *The New Enclosure: The Appropriation of Public Land in Neoliberal Britain.* London: Verso.
2. Rao, V. 2009. Embracing urbanism: The city as archive. *New Literary History* 40(2), 380.
3. Burgum, S. 2020. This city is an archive: Squatting history and urban authority. *Journal of Urban History* 48(3), 504–22.
4. Reeve, K. 2015. Criminalising the poor: Squatting, homelessness, and social welfare. In L. Fox O'Mahony, D. O'Mahony and R. Hickey (eds) *Moral Rhetoric and the Criminalisation of Squatting: Vulnerable Demons?* Abingdon: Routledge, p. 150.
5. Blomley, N. 2004. *Unsettling the City: Urban Land and the Politics of Property.* Abingdon: Routledge.
6. Bhandar, B. 2018. *Colonial Lives of Property: Law, Land, and Racial Regimes of Ownership.* Durham, NC: Duke University Press.
7. Blomley, *Unsettling the City.*
8. Powell, R. 2013. The theoretical concept of the 'civilising offensive' (*Beschavings-soffensief*): Notes on its origins and uses. *Human Figurations* 2(2).
9. Cockburn, P., Bruun, M., Risager, B., and Thorup, M. 2018. Introduction: Disagreement as a window onto property. In Bruun, M., Cockburn, P., Risager, B., and Thorup, M. (eds) *Contested Property Claims: What Disagreement Tells Us about Ownership.* Abingdon: Routledge, p. xi.
10. Blomley, N. 2016. The boundaries of property: Complexity, relationality and spatiality. *Law and Society Review* 50(1), 593–4.
11. *The Guardian.* 2024. Fewer than one in 10 arts workers in the UK have working-class roots. www.theguardian.com/inequality/article/2024/may/18/arts-workers-uk-working-class-roots-cultural-sector-diversity.
12. United Nations. 2019. Make cities and human settlements inclusive, safe, resilient and sustainable. https://unstats.un.org/sdgs/report/2019/goal-11/
13. Simone, A. 2004. *For the City Yet to Come: Changing African Life in Four Cities.* Durham, NC: Duke University Press, p. 215.
14. Ibid. p. 2.
15. Ibid. p. 2.
16. Ibid. p. 9.
17. Ibid. p. 16.
18. Ibid. p. 214.
19. McFarlane, C. 2018. Fragment urbanism: Politics at the margins of the city. *Environment and Planning D: Society and Space* 36(6), 1012.
20. AlSayyad, N. and Roy, A. 2004. Urban informality: Crossing borders. In A. Roy and N. AlSayyad (eds) *Urban Informality: Transnational Perspectives from the Middle East, Latin America, and South Asia.* Lanham, MD: Lexington Books, p. 5.

21. Perlman, J. 2004. Marginality: From myth to reality in the favelas of Rio de Janeiro, 1969–2002. In Roy and AlSayyad (eds) *Urban Informality*, p. 120.
22. Roy, A. 2004. Transnational trespassings. In Roy and AlSayyad (eds) *Urban Informality*, p. 311.
23. Yiftachl, O. and Yakobi, H. 2004. Control, resistance, and informality: Urban ethnocracy in Beer-Sheva, Israel. In Roy and AlSayyad (eds) *Urban Informality*, p. 218.
24. Jaffe, R. and Koster, M. 2019. The myth of formality in the global North: Informality-as-innovation in Dutch governance. *International Journal of Urban and Regional Research* 43(3), 563–8.

Index

Thanks to our Patreon subscriber:

Ciaran Kane

Who has shown generosity and
comradeship in support of our publishing.

Check out the other perks you get by subscribing
to our Patreon – visit patreon.com/plutopress.
Subscriptions start from £3 a month.

The Pluto Press Newsletter

Hello friend of Pluto!

Want to stay on top of the best radical books we publish?

Then sign up to be the first to hear about our new books, as well as special events, podcasts and videos.

You'll also get 50% off your first order with us when you sign up.

Come and join us!

Go to bit.ly/PlutoNewsletter